Exploring Ezra

The secret of spiritual success

DayOne

© Day One Publications 2004
First printed 2004

ISBN 1 903087 63-5

9 781903 087633

British Library Cataloguing in Publication Data available

Published by Day One Publications
P O Box 66, Leominster, HR6 0XB
☎ 01568 613 740 FAX 01568 611 473
email—sales@dayone.co.uk
web site—www.dayone.co.uk
North American—e-mail-sales@dayonebookstore.com
North American web site—www.dayonebookstore.com

Designed by Steve Devane and printed by CPD

To
My Dear Wife
Ber
'Her children arise and call her blessed; her husband also, and he praises her: "Many women do noble things, but you surpass them all."'
(Proverbs 31:28–29)

Contents

Introduction

One might well ask where Exploring Ezra fits in with existing commentaries and other expository material. Perhaps the best way to answer that question is to give a brief account of its history. This work began as an exposition of Ezra 7:10: 'For Ezra had devoted himself to the study and observance of the Law of the LORD, and to teaching its decrees and laws in Israel.' Pondering these words presented the possibility of a short series of three or perhaps four sermons. When a preacher selects a verse of Scripture as his text he feels a great responsibility to ensure that he has not taken it out of context. Thus due regard for the relevant circumstances, setting, and historical genre, presented other theological themes that demanded attention. For example, Ezra is primarily a book that presents the sovereign God superintending history. This theme is a backdrop to the Ezra 7:10 text. Soon it became evident that there was something of immense worth in each chapter that had a contemporary resonance. This work, therefore, emerged from a series of sermons, based on selected verses, from each of the ten chapters of the book of Ezra.

This brief outline of the origin and development of the work will explain why it does not include a survey of the critical issues in the body of the work. In omitting them one is not suggesting that they are unimportant. The process which every preacher must go through in sermon preparation whereby issues must be addressed pertaining to the complexity of sources, composition and date (which are issues of particular relevance to Ezra), needs to be set aside (not ignored) in the interest of instruction and edification.

This work seeks to present a clear and relevant understanding of the meaning and application of the book of Ezra for the contemporary Christian without getting bogged down in issues pertaining to critical scholarship. The approach taken, therefore, has been to focus on a theological perspective that aims to edify and instruct. This book, consequently, is inspired by pastoral concern to see people brought to mature faith. As such it is devotional in nature with an emphasis on contemporary and timeless relevance and application. It was primarily prepared for and presented to believers. Hence, each chapter presupposes a firm commitment to the authority of Scripture as divine revelation.

Every preacher knows the frustration of turning to a commentary for help and finding fine technical detail but little spiritual insight. Scholarship has merit but there is a great need for expository material that is more accessible. Scholarship may work in harmony with faith. The botanist, poet and Englishman may each see different things when they look at a red rose. One would expect the perspective of the botanist to be primarily scientific and the perception of the poet to be essentially creative. The Englishman's understanding of the same object might well include nationalist sentiment as he sees a symbolic significance in a way that is (perhaps) different to the poet. Although it is possible to have an Englishman who is a professional botanist with an appreciation for poetry! The point is that each (botanist, poet and Englishman) would produce different works on the same object (the rose). It would be peculiar if all three dimensions (scientific, aesthetic and symbolic) were represented in one work. In this sense one perspective does not make another invalid and it is only when all perspectives are presented that we can have a comprehensive appreciation of the subject. This work seeks to present a perspective that is somewhat neglected in other works.

We need to be careful that some issues, such as suspicion about the authorship of Ezra, do not lead to scepticism about its authority. For example, the idea that Ezra was merely the figment of a chronicler's imagination is a theory that undermines the credibility of the book only if we lose sight of the fact that the real author of the book is the Holy Spirit! Similarly the view that the present order of the book is the result of mistakes by later copyists can result in people becoming disillusioned with the Bible. *Exploring Ezra* is intended to present the theological issues of the text in a way that is readable and challenging. If literary and historical considerations lead one to believe that the text of Scripture is deficient or distorted then there is a problem with such an approach. One can legitimately believe in the historical Ezra, despite what some works assert.

One theory concerning authorship suggests that the book may be attributed to a young man (an admirer) who was a contemporary of Ezra.

According to this opinion, Ezra was written many years after the events it records as an idealised account for edification purposes. Within this matrix the historical veracity of Ezra is questionable because the work is seen, not as an attempt to convey the history of the period, but to present a legend which has been liberally embellished. The fact that the account is written (mostly) in the first person is not taken to indicate its autobiographical nature but merely as a common literary device of the time. These and other issues are the scaffolding of scholarship, which the preacher often finds has to be dismantled in order to present the edifice of the text as it ought to be seen.

Is the book of Ezra the work of a single author? Is it autobiographical and historical or is it legend serving propaganda purposes? These and similar questions are, historically, raised in the critical analysis of the book. Perhaps Ezra was written in order to report progress in relation to the commission entrusted to him by the Persian emperor, but there is no consensus on this and other matters where more problems are raised than resolved.

Our starting point is: *'All Scripture is God-breathed and is useful for teaching, rebuking, correcting and training in righteousness, so that the man of God may be thoroughly equipped for every good work'* (2 Tim. 3:16). We want, therefore, to search this book for its doctrines rather than its difficulties. Much has been written that engages in defining difficulties that are then either denied or defended by others. It is interesting to learn from history that Persian kings had a policy of supporting local religious practices, but if that information is deemed to be necessary to prove the validity of the biblical account then the approach is seriously flawed. Let history stand or fall on the basis of the biblical account and not the reverse!

This work is essentially an exegetical and theological discourse of the biblical themes in the book of Ezra. The diverse views of scholars concerning literary and historical issues are interesting but irrelevant to its primary aim, which is to present a readable and challenging interpretation of the message of Ezra.

We should neither be unaware of the critical issues nor uninterested in them, but the foremost concern in these pages is to present the book of Ezra as the Word of God. The critical issues are, therefore, subordinate to the theological thrust of the text. Ezra is both autobiographical and historical in nature and where other views contribute to that clarity they are to be welcomed.

Secular history has been subject to revision in such a way that there is no longer any single, universal understanding or acceptance of historical data. In our postmodern society it has become a kaleidoscopic image that depends on how one twists and rearranges the issues to suit ones own class, culture and convictions. Is this a healthy way to look at biblical history? We must not become detached from our moorings or go to sea without compass or anchor.

The historical issues of Ezra have a theological dimension. It is a book that establishes the legitimacy of a distinct community to be the sole successors of Solomon's Temple, but that does not make it anti-Samaritan propaganda. We need to regain a sense of perspective by reminding ourselves that the books of Ezra and Nehemiah are the most important sources for the history of Judah in the post-exilic period. Other sources are virtually insignificant by comparison. This history provides a backdrop to God's dealings with his people. The purpose of the book is not to give us insight into the society of the period but to convey the spiritual issues of importance. Our telescope, therefore, will zoom in on the theological issues.

Undeniably there are difficulties and unanswered questions relating to composition, date, history, sources, literary analysis etc. but in the absence of material that would definitively resolve such issues we should have sufficient humility to be content with limited knowledge. Speculation fills the vacuum created by the absence of such humility. We need to understand that the respective chronological order of Ezra and Nehemiah are less important than the theological concerns of these books. Theories may be unsupported and conjectural or adequately argued and explained in other works that either undermine or underpin faith, but this work seeks to put material into the hands of God's people that will challenge and encourage them.

Ezra gives thanks to God for 'a wall of protection in Judah and Jerusalem' (9:9). Some have suggested that this is proof that when Ezra arrived in Jerusalem he found the walls already built by Nehemiah. This has clear implications for the chronological order of the writing of these books. What are we to make of it? It appears incongruous. Consider for a moment that Limerick City in Ireland was once (during its Norman period) a walled city. The locals today still speak of the 'walls of Limerick' and they are mentioned in literary and historical sources. However, there are no 'walls of Limerick'! All that remains of those walls are a few ruins. Nevertheless those remnants exist in sufficient quantity in various locations to serve as an accurate outline of the ancient city. Is it possible that Ezra was referring to the remnants of the walls in a manner that indicated his awareness that the boundaries of a distinct territory were marked out by fragments of walls, which constituted in his mind, a perimeter?

This view is complimented rather than contradicted by scholars who see that the 'wall of protection' is not to be understood as a wall like that of Jericho. It is rather more like a fence around a vineyard. Its primary purpose is to define a territory rather than protect it from invasion. But in defining such an area one is giving to it a certain legal status. In any case, whatever we conclude about a wall of protection in Jerusalem there could not have been a wall surrounding Judah! The Authorised Version is closer to the literal translation of the verse when it says, '... God ... *hath extended mercy unto us...to give us a wall in Judah and Jerusalem.'* It is not certain from this tense that the wall has already been given.

We begin with the book of Ezra as part of the canon of Scripture. To say that it might have been constructed differently ultimately does not really matter. If there was an editor (or more than one) who could have selected different source material and arranged it differently it makes no difference now to the reality of the book as it exists today. The present arrangement of the book presents its central concerns.

Ezra is a narrative that centres on the redemptive history of God's people and it is best understood as a work that seeks to portray this. It is about political emancipation, geographical relocation, spiritual restoration and religious reorganisation. Ezra was a reformer working to God's blueprint. He sought the re-establishment of the pre-exilic status (religious, institutional, territorial and, perhaps, political). He worked toward seeing the altar and temple re-built, the reintroduction of sacrifices and the observance of feasts in their true spirit. He worked toward preserving the religious identity of God's people in accordance with the clear commands of God's Word, particularly in relation to the prohibition of mixed marriages and forbidding unholy associations.

There are things that we do not know about the man Ezra. For example we are not explicitly told anything of his secular status. Nevertheless, verse twenty-five of chapter seven reveals something of the scope of his moral and vested authority.

Ezra is a book that emphasises the ongoing work of God with his people to preserve, protect and promote his redemptive purposes. The narrative is sometimes organised more thematically than chronologically but it is always a reverent appreciation of the gracious outworking of the divine will. As such it becomes much more intelligible when it is understood as theological narrative.

There is a continuity of God's purpose evident in Ezra. The temple was the central institution of the Judaic faith and forms of worship prior to the Babylonian exile. The rebuilding of the altar and the temple clearly indicate the desire to re-establish the old order. The plans for the new temple replicated the older one in both dimension and method of construction (compare Ezra 6:3 ff. and 1 Kings 6:2 ff.). The vessels used in the second temple were the very ones which Nebuchadnezzar had carried off to Babylon and which Cyrus had returned. The return of the vessels is a significant act in the process of restoration. Nebuchadnezzar had put these vessels 'in the temple of his god' (1:7). That was an act of subjugation meant to emphasise the superiority of the Babylonian gods to the subordinate Jewish deity. The return of the vessels, therefore, emphasises the act of restoration. Similarly, the genealogical lists serve to emphasise continuity in personnel. The dedication of the second temple evokes memories of Solomon's Temple (1 Kings 8). The desire to preserve the genealogical purity of the people stresses continuity by suggesting that the old community is reconstituted in the new. Words like 'return' and 'exile' reinforce the idea that a dispossessed people are repossessing a particular territory. They are going home.

The return from Babylonian exile is represented as a second exodus in Ezra and the hand of God is seen in the historical process, even in the detail of the day of departure (see Ezra 7:9 and Ex. 12:2,40–42). In all of this Ezra re-establishes that sense of identity in the community, that they are a people through whom God has commenced to work out his purposes on earth. As such it serves to remind them of the continuity of such purposes by emphasising the relationship between God and his chosen people.

Ezra acknowledges that the Persian emperor took the initiative in sanctioning and supporting the exodus (7:27–28; 9:9). As such he is identified as a significant agent in the outworking of God's eternal purposes. However, it is not clear if Ezra and the post-exilic community saw their repatriation as the first phase in a process that would ultimately lead to the re-establishment of the Davidic monarchy and all that it promised. It is hard to imagine how they could have envisaged it otherwise with such an emphasis on the Pentateuch where those promises are clearly expressed. Ultimately they did move toward political independence that necessitated the overthrow of foreign domination. The opposition that they encountered from local officials may be an indication that their regional opponents recognised the deep-seated desire of the Jewish people to move toward political independence under their own king.

Although the Persian kings are portrayed positively, their local officials are not. They are presented as a form of opposition to the will of God by their interfering and attempts at undermining the work of reconstruction. The apologetic emphasis of the book exposes their accusations of sedition as a malicious misrepresentation because desire and determination to achieve this end had not yet met. In illustrating that their problems stemmed from corrupt local officials and not the Persian court, Ezra emphasises loyalty to the imperial power.

We would be wrong to assume that their policy of separation was merely an expedient response to the political problems encountered at a local level. Their isolationist attitudes came from a re-awakening of understanding concerning their unique identity. They clearly understood that their neighbours were outside the covenant relationship and this is reflected in their refusal to be identified with them (4:1–2). Similarly their position on marriage (9:1–2) is one that seeks to protect and preserve that unique identity. They were to be a holy (separate) people. Whatever relationship they desired to have with the neighbouring community, a policy of integration certainly did not feature in it. They did not want to be assimilated into the culture, subjugated to it or supplanted by it. Their freedom was a freedom from such things. Now they had a glorious opportunity to practice their faith and they were determined to do that without entering into unholy alliances with others even if that meant incurring the suspicion and hostility of their neighbours.

Perhaps this could be viewed as a rather unattractive aspect of their religion, but in our age of ecumenism and inter-faith endeavour the people of God would do well to rediscover that sense of uniqueness. We are to love our neighbours (even, and especially, those who would constitute the modern equivalent of the Samaritan). However, we are to do so without compromising our spiritual integrity. They preserved their unique identity against overwhelming odds by their unequivocal attitude to protecting religious purity. We are not to be monastic in mindset and cloistered away from the community. We are called to live in the world but not to allow the ways of the world to influence us. On the contrary, we have an obligation to influence the world. The people of God must be prepared, therefore, to say no to community when it becomes compromising and no to integration when it becomes infidelity and no to so-called neighbourliness when it negates the distinctiveness of God's people. Preserving their unique identity was a matter of obedience to God and not merely a peculiar interpretation of the law. They were merely saying yes to Yahweh! They did not consummate a relationship with the community because they did not want to be consumed by it.

Ezra did not introduce new laws rather he emphasised the existing law. There is no evidence to warrant the view that his was a peculiar interpretation, rather it was a matter of practical application. The 'law' to which 7:10 refers is probably the Pentateuch, as we know it. Apparent discrepancies between the text of the Pentateuch and portions cited in Ezra may legitimately be attributed to Ezra's preaching where the Word was explained, expounded and interpreted in a manner that emphasised its contemporary application.

We must be careful about what some scholars say and be more like the Bereans who tested the accuracy of Paul's claims by searching the Scriptures for themselves in order to establish the validity of his assertions (Acts 17:10–12). For example, Williamson says 'marriage with foreigners in itself was not forbidden in the Mosaic law...'[1] This statement is inaccurate because it is expressly forbidden in Deuteronomy: *'When the LORD your God brings you into the land you are entering to possess and drives out before you many nations...Make no treaty with them...Do not intermarry with them. Do not give your daughters to their sons or take their daughters for your sons'* (7:1–3). The reason is clearly stated: *'For they will turn your sons away from following me to serve other gods'* (Deut. 7:4). Psalm 106 catalogues the evil practices of God's people throughout their turbulent history and says, *'They mingled with the nations and adopted their customs'* (v. 35). Williamson cites references that deal with the giving of Hagar to Abram by Sarai and the marriages of Joseph and Moses as examples of the acceptability of such marriages. These marriages were acceptable, but exceptional, and we must remember that the exception does not prove the principle. It is true that Miriam and Aaron were rebuked for talking against Moses because he had a Cushite wife, indeed Miriam was smitten with leprosy (Num. 12). It is also true that Scripture does not condemn such marriages and, therefore, we must not be begrudging in our admission that God condones them. Though it would not be entirely inappropriate to have reservations about the morality of Abraham's relationship with Hagar. However, the Deuteronomy instruction not to intermarry was given so that it would prevail in the post-exilic circumstances when the people of God came to inhabit the Promised Land. It did not apply, therefore, to Abram, Moses or Joseph but it came into effect later and certainly applied to the post-Babylonian period. It cannot, therefore, be argued that Ezra's view of intermarriage was his own peculiar interpretation of the law.

Exploring Ezra takes a path that allows us to encounter the diverse landscapes and extraordinary terrain of this biblical book. In it we may learn as much about our society and ourselves as we do about Ezra and his. It emphasises the sovereignty of God in superintending history and affectionately guiding his people toward the fulfilment of his purposes. It should instil a sense of appreciation for that providential care which we receive from his gracious hand. The authority of Scripture and the necessity for preaching are keynote themes. We are reminded that God is the architect and builder of the church and that although there may be opposition to that work, his will is never thwarted and his purposes prevail. We are exhorted to trust the truth and to see things from a heavenly perspective and avoid compromise. We are reminded of that sense of urgency that should attend the Lord's work and the necessity for a true understanding of unity that is discerning about the inherent dangers in proposals for partnership. The story of Ezra is part of the bigger story of the Bible, which is about the history of redemption and the last chapter of that story is still being written.

Christ is the golden thread in this tapestry. Thus the sovereignty of God in superintending history is directed toward Calvary as the pivotal and climactic event in the history of the world. Events are still moving toward an inexorable eschatological outcome and Ezra is part of that narrative. The precision of God's providences are truly remarkable, but the most astonishing of all is that in the fullness of time the pre-incarnate Christ took on human flesh and entered our fallen world as the Christ of those who will be saved. In examining passages of Ezra that are sometimes seen as a tedious list of names we are reminded that the Lord keeps a list of names in the Lamb's book of life.

We are exhorted to consider our superficial giving to God in the light of his sacrificial love in laying down his life for our redemption. We see the undivided urgency of God's people in the promising post-exilic period and it inspires us in this generation to face the urgency of our commission. We are asked where we stand in terms of lamenting or lauding labour for the Lord. In considering union, uniformity, and unity we must not just reflect *on* the issue of unity but actually reflect it *in* our relationships within the household of faith, while avoiding all that pretends to be unity when it is not.

We find help in overcoming opposition by following the example of Jesus: 'Consider him who endured such opposition from sinful men, so that you will not grow weary and lose heart' (Heb. 12:3).

In times of trouble we need to adhere to the teaching of the Word and take up our trowels and labour for God. Teaching is central to discipleship as Christ proved in his teaching ministry to his disciples. Preaching is central to the success of our mission, as it was central to the ministry of Christ who preached for progress in his disciples. In these chapters we learn, too, that God protects and guides his beloved.

The study of Scripture is a crucial necessity for the believer. Again we come back to Jesus and see that although he was raised in an obscure location he learned and taught the Scriptures. This is reflected in both his temptation in the wilderness and teaching in the synagogues. In considering the relationship between practice and preaching, Christ is our supreme model, but Ezra, as a hero of history, also presents us with lessons in leadership.

Ezra had a true heavenly perspective that was evident in the way he was appalled by the apostasy of God's people. We, too, ought to be a people who are astonished by the abandonment of biblical perspective by God's people today.

In the final chapter, 'Contrition, Confession and the Cost of Compromise', we are brought to the foot of the cross once again and realise that we can never stray far from its shadow without needing the grace it supplies.

The questions at the end of each chapter should stimulate further reflection and discussion.

Footnote

1 **Williamson, H.G.M.,** *Word Biblical Commentary, Ezra and Nehemiah,* p. 130.

The sovereign God superintending history

Bible reading

The book of Ezra: An overview

It is good to be reminded of the historicity of the Bible, that it is not just fable or folklore. With this thought in mind consider the following series of events which enable us to see the hand of God in history. In 586 BC Jerusalem fell and the captivity of Judah seemed complete. This marked the third and final deportation to Babylon. But in 539 BC Cyrus, leader of the Persian Empire, conquered Babylon.

The Persians had an entirely different philosophy to the Babylonians. This is worthy of mention because it enables us to see God at work in the broad sweep of history. When the Babylonians were in power their philosophy was to attack, ransack and take people captive to Babylon. The Persians, however, allowed people to return to their homelands. Thus the different ethnic groups, including the Jews, were permitted to go back to their land and develop as separate nations under Persia's leadership.

At the time of the Babylonian captivity the hope of emancipation may have seemed strange with not even the remotest possibility of fulfilment. There is a tendency for God's people at difficult times to judge God's Word in the light of circumstances. This is always flawed because it does not allow for God's eternal and unchanging power. We sometimes let events interpret God's Word rather than allowing God's Word to explain events!

Eternal perspective

The book of Ezra gives us an eternal perspective by setting apparently secular events in spiritual context. Thus it enables us to see that God is sovereign and is never outsmarted nor outmanoeuvred. He can cause empires to do his bidding and orchestrate events to the fulfilment of his own will (Eph. 1:11–12).

Cyrus grants permission for the return to Jerusalem, and Sheshbazzar heads up the first group of returnees. Zerubbabel leads in building the altar and beginning the work of rebuilding the Temple. In 522 BC King Darius comes to the throne and reigns until 486 BC. It is during his reign that the temple is finally completed, and it is into that setting that we read of Haggai and Zechariah prophesying. Darius had died and a new king came to the throne (Artaxerxes, 464–423 BC). It was during his reign that Ezra led the return to establish temple worship. We see in the book of Ezra that God moves the nations to do as he decrees!

Opposition to the work of God

There was opposition to the work of God. Cyrus had given a decree that allowed the Jews to go back and rebuild the temple. That opposition came from the governor of the Trans-Euphrates and others associated with him. We should note that wherever God is at work there will be opposition but ultimately God will prevail. His plans and purposes will never be thwarted no matter how bleak the situation may appear.

'*But the eye of their God was upon the elders of the Jews, so that they could not make them cease till a report could go to Darius. Then a written answer was returned concerning this matter*' (5:5 NKJV). These words present us with the elementary truth that in spite of opposition God watches over his own because there is that special relationship of belonging! It was true for the people of God then and it is true for every child of God now.

Certain people who opposed the work wrote to the Emperor in Persia saying that the Jews had always been troublesome and that he should investigate their allegation. So the king had the records checked and they corroborated the complaint. Consequently, the work ceased for a while. Then they wrote off again and a search was made to find the initial decree from Cyrus that the work should be done. That second search of the chronicles revealed that in the year 520 Cyrus decreed that the people could rebuild. So permission was granted again. Then we read, '*Now therefore, Tattenai, governor of the region beyond the River, and Shethar-Boznai, and your companions the Persians who are beyond the River, keep yourselves far from there'* (Ezra 6:6 NKJV). It is extraordinary that such a memorandum was sent back to the troublemakers. They were instructed not only to stay away (the modern day equivalent of a barring order) and cease their hostility, but in addition they were told to contribute to the rebuilding costs! They overstepped themselves and their scheme backfired.

It is instructive for us to note that although enemies of the gospel will oppose and frustrate they will never succeed in stopping the building of the church. *'I will build my church, and the gates of Hades will not overcome it'* (Matt.16:18). Imagine some of God's people wondering why they had returned to rubble and trouble. Are we not sometimes like that? There may be times when we wonder why we ever embarked on this or that spiritual project! It is a spiritual battle but we are victorious in Christ! The devil oversteps the mark and God causes even Satan's wicked schemes to please him and fall in with his plans. As we read on we learn that the work continued and prospered under the encouraging preaching of Haggai and Zechariah: *'So the elders of the Jews built, and they prospered through the prophesying of Haggai the prophet and Zechariah the son of Iddo. And they built and finished it, according to the commandment of the God of Israel, and according to the command of Cyrus, Darius, and Artaxerxes king of Persia'* (6:14 NKJV). Encouragement came through the Word of God.

God works even opposition to his advantage

One of the abiding lessons of this book is that God works even opposition to his advantage. He is in control so that what has commenced will continue unhindered until completion. In these days there is opposition and much discouragement along the way, but there is also great encouragement from the Word.

Notice when Ezra returned to the homeland that the people assembled together, a fast was proclaimed and they humbly petitioned their God for protection. There is an important pattern here for any community of God's people. The importance of assembling together at the appointed times cannot be over-stressed. There was a huge project in front of them that caused them to meet together. They prayed and petitioned God because they recognised that what lay before them was difficult. Nevertheless they were going to stand up and be counted. They didn't dare embark on such a project without preparing themselves.

God's people today face the daunting task of fulfilling the Great Commission. Modern thinking and moral standards are against us, but the gracious hand of God is upon us as it was upon his people when he navigated the nation by engaging Ezra. For our part we need to do what the people of God in Ezra's time did. They met together, humbled themselves, cried out to God, petitioned him and fasted. There was seriousness in seeking after God. How many of us know that kind of earnestness? May God equip us and may his gracious hand be upon us.

Questions: for discussion

1. What do you understand by the phrase 'the sovereignty of God'?
2. How can a biblical understanding of God's sovereignty bring comfort and confidence to the committed Christian? See Rom. 8:28.
3. Is God involved in world affairs today? See Matt. 5:13–16. Discuss the implications of these verses for the believer.
4. How can our understanding of the way God 'stirred up the spirit of Cyrus' inspire us to pray? See 1 Tim. 2:1–4.
5. What are the situations in the world for which we should pray today?
6. What advice would you give to a Christian who feels forsaken by God?

The precision of God's providence

Bible reading: Ezra 1

Focus on ...

'In the first year of Cyrus king of Persia, in order to fulfil the word of the LORD spoken by Jeremiah, the LORD moved the heart of Cyrus king of Persia to make a proclamation throughout his realm and to put it in writing.' (Ezra 1:1)

The AV says that the Lord '...stirred up the spirit of Cyrus king of Persia...'

These words draw attention to the fact that the events recorded in Ezra occur at a particular point in time and relate to a specific place and person. Here, in other words, is a historical reference to a secular ruler in the ancient world. The time is very significant in the history of Israel, as it is the point at which a remnant of God's people return from seventy years of captivity in Babylon to rebuild the temple in Jerusalem.

God stirs the human heart

It is a truly remarkable opening to the book of Ezra that the Lord *'stirred up the spirit of Cyrus.'* The Lord moved the heart of this heathen ruler of a heathen people to do his bidding at the appointed time.

Before we proceed any further let us take a look at other instances in Scripture where this expression, 'stir', is used. In a passage that speaks of the sin and consequent conquest of the Reubenites, the Gadites and the half-tribe of Manasseh we read these words:

'But they were unfaithful to the God of their fathers and prostituted themselves to the gods of the peoples of the land, whom God had destroyed before them. So the God of Israel stirred up the spirit of Pul king of Assyria…who took [them]…into exile…' (1 Chron. 5:25–26).

Obviously God can use the princes of this world as puppets to progress his purposes. He engages the mind, will and passions of people to fulfil his plans. Even though the actors in the overall drama of history may be merely seeking to prosper their own programme of ambitions, God is at work behind the scenes. In Haggai chapter one we read these words: *'Then Haggai, the LORD's messenger, gave this message of the LORD to the people: "I am with you," declares the LORD. So the LORD stirred up the spirit of Zerubbabel son of Shealtiel, governor of Judah, and the spirit of Joshua son of Jehozadak, the high priest, and the spirit of the whole remnant of the people. They came and began to work on the house of the LORD Almighty, their God, on the twenty-fourth day of the sixth month in the second year of King Darius'* (vv. 13–15). It was Zerubbabel who led the first return from Babylonian captivity and he did so because the almighty God of heaven *'stirred up'* his spirit. In Acts we read of Paul in Athens: *'While Paul was waiting for them in Athens, he was greatly distressed to see that the city was full of idols'* (Acts 17:16). The AV puts it like this: *'while Paul waited for them at Athens his spirit was stirred in him, when he saw the city wholly given to idolatry.'* Later in that chapter we see that Paul's spirit was so grieved by this idolatry that he was moved to explain the truth of the gospel. Paul was so passionate about the truth of the gospel that idolatry distressed him. May our spirits be stirred within us to grieve at the sight of the idolatry that surrounds us! It is the Holy Spirit who quickens the spirits of men and so may the Holy Spirit not only stir our souls but also move our mouths to speak of him.

The fulfilment of prophecy

The decree of Cyrus was the fulfilment of prophecy. Cyrus was predestined to come to power. In Isaiah God speaks to his people through his servant Isaiah to remind them that he is the Lord and all that that implies in terms of being in control of circumstances. In chapter forty-four the people are reminded of their redemptive relationship to him. He speaks to them not only as the majestic and almighty creator of this vast universe, but as their creator. He invites them to contemplate the awesome thought that it is such a one as he that has been involved in their lives even before they were born. Thus we read, *'This is what the LORD says—your Redeemer, who formed you in the womb: "I am the LORD, who has made all things, who alone stretched out the heavens, who spread out the earth by myself "'* (v. 24). Then God proceeds to tell them that he, the one with such power, authorises the words of the prophets and guarantees their fulfilment: *'Who carries out the words of his servants and fulfils the predictions of his messengers'* (v. 26).

We learn that the one with such power has very specific and very special purposes for his people: 'who says of Jerusalem, "It shall be inhabited," of the towns of Judah, "They shall be built," and of their ruins, "I will restore them,"' (v. 26). Then we come to the astonishing words: 'who says of Cyrus, "He is my shepherd and will accomplish all that I please; he will say of Jerusalem, 'Let it be rebuilt,' and of the temple, 'Let its foundations be laid.'"' (v. 28). When we consider the fact that these words preceded Cyrus' decree by about two centuries it is truly astonishing! Cyrus was an instrument in God's hands which he used to promote his plans. Thus we read in chapter forty-five, 'This is what the LORD says to his anointed, to Cyrus, whose right hand I take hold of to subdue nations before him and to strip kings of their armour, to open doors before him so that gates will not be shut' (v. 1). God's purposes will not be obstructed and nothing is strong enough to stand in his way: 'I will go before you and will level the mountains; I will break down gates of bronze and cut through bars of iron' (v. 2). God will demonstrate his power in such a way that it will reinvigorate the faith of his people 'so that you may know that I am the LORD, the God of Israel, who summons you by name' (v. 3). In doing this marvellous thing he will demonstrate his authority on earth and in heaven so that people will be without excuse if they do not yield allegiance to him. Thus we read, 'so that from the rising of the sun to the place of its setting men may know there is none besides me. I am the LORD, and there is no other' (v. 6). The mighty emperor, Cyrus, is merely a puppet to do the bidding of God: 'I will raise up Cyrus in my righteousness: I will make all his ways straight. He will rebuild my city and set my exiles free' (v. 13).

These words are dated approximately two hundred years before Cyrus issued his decree that allowed for the repatriation of God's people to

Jerusalem. This is a wonderful passage of Scripture that speaks of the almighty power of God. It is all the more remarkable in the very specific nature of its prophetic content. Cyrus is named as the one who would be used of God to achieve his ends. We get a picture of a majestic God who is orchestrating events to a very specific and detailed plan. The redemptive purposes of God are being forwarded by one with whom nothing is impossible so that when the time is right his plans will succeed.

The redemptive purposes of God

When the fullness of time had come the Lord Jesus Christ entered this world in the form of human flesh to fulfil the redemptive purposes of God. He set his face as a flint toward Jerusalem so that the will of the Father would be accomplished at Calvary. He rose on the third day in accordance with the redemptive plan so that death might have no more dominion over those who are washed in his blood and trusting in that completed work. For he declared that it is finished and who are we to say otherwise? He ascended into heaven where he is seated at the right hand of the Father there to make intercession for us. He has called us by name, our names are written in the Lamb's book of life in the indelible ink of His precious blood. Just as the names of the people of Israel were borne on the breastplate of the high priest, Jesus is our great high priest, the only mediator between God and man and he bears our names on his heart before the heavenly Father. All is being done in the fullness of time and all to his ultimate glory. The great architect of the universe is working according to schedule. It is as if God keeps a diary and certain appointments will be met.

The role of Cyrus in the affairs of God was to liberate the Jews from Babylonian captivity. God deposited within him a desire and a determination to execute his will. At the end of Daniel chapter five we read of the death of Belshazzar, king of the Chaldeans and the emergence of Darius, the Mede. God is governing global affairs in accordance with his blueprint for mankind. And so Ezra opens with this decree of Cyrus seventy years after the first Jewish captives were taken to Babylon.

Jeremiah prophesied a seventy-year Babylonian captivity as a punishment for habitual disobedience. In chapter twenty-five of Jeremiah we are told the reason for the period of captivity and the means by which it will come about: 'Therefore the LORD Almighty says this: *"Because you have not listened to my words, I will summon all the peoples of the north and my servant Nebuchadnezzar king of Babylon,"* declares the LORD, *"and I will bring them against this land and its inhabitants and against all the surrounding nations. I will completely destroy them and make them an object of horror and scorn, and an everlasting ruin"'* (vv. 8–9). We read of the terrible outcome of Israel's contempt for the Word of God and we are told how long this period of desolation will last: *'This whole country will become a desolate wasteland, and these nations will serve the king of Babylon seventy years'* (v. 11).

So the reason for God's punishment is made clear and the duration of their captivity is specified. This message is restated a few chapters on, *'This is what the LORD says: "When seventy years are completed for Babylon, I will come to you and fulfil my gracious promise to bring you back to this place"'* (29:10). Again it must be stated that these words were spoken many years before the events of which they speak occurred (approx.150 years).

Patience and perspective

Isn't it true that the purposes of God seem to move slowly, slower perhaps than we would like? We sometimes lack patience, understanding and perspective. In our own experience one of the most difficult places to be is that place between the promise and its fulfilment. It is in such times and places that our faith is tested and trained. God moves to his agenda and his timeframe, not ours! But we may be confident of this: God's purposes are never abandoned, thwarted, delayed, derailed or diverted. I wonder if you have ever had the experience of catching a bus that arrived late and then had to take an alternative route because of road works. The detour has knock-on effects and when you disembark you are already late for an appointment and find you have to walk some distance to your destination. Well God's plans are not subject to those kinds of frustrations. His purposes follow the route determined in accordance with the timetable of heaven. There are no delays and no diversions as his purposes are always on time and on target!

This account in Ezra of the return of the remnant of God's people demonstrates the glorious truth that God is sovereign. In spite of how things may appear the Lord is in control. He is not an abstract or impersonal force. Although he is supremely powerful, wise and holy he is also gracious and merciful. We see his very essence in the incarnate Christ.

The captain is in control

There is a story about a ship at sea in a storm. The passengers are fearful that they are in perilous danger that the vessel may sink. A group of passengers are huddled together and in a state of distress when somebody suggests that one of the party should go and talk to the captain. The elected person makes his way to the helm of the ship where he sees the captain from a distance. He moves towards him and as he does so he catches a glimpse of the captain's face. Immediately his fears are quelled because he has seen on the captain's face the serenity of a man who has nothing to fear. It is obvious that everything is under control. Oh, how we need to catch sight of the face of the captain of our salvation. The one who is at the helm of our souls is the one we have been reading about in Isaiah who created the heavens and the earth. May we be able to declare with confidence those words of Paul, 'I know whom I have believed, and am convinced that he is able to guard what I have entrusted to him for that day' (2 Tim. 1:12).

I remember when I was a child that an armchair caught fire at home. I don't know how this happened; perhaps it was a spark from the fire in the grate. However, this was in the days before fire-retardant fabric and the upholstery and the chair were ablaze. My poor mother panicked and tried to douse it with water and made a terrific noise shrieking for help, which instilled more fear in my little trembling heart. I was motionless with fright. I thought the house would be burned to the ground for sure. But when all seemed lost my father stepped into the room. A giant in my eyes, he lifted the chair in his arms and strode into the garden with it. He suffered some minor burns but he had saved our home from destruction. It was a heroic deed borne out of love for his family. But just think of our precious Saviour and his love for those who are his own. If he laid down his life to save you will he not also use all his might to protect you and preserve you? Our heavenly father steps into the most distressing situations and ministers peace and hope through his mighty strength.

His promises are perfectly and precisely fulfilled

The truth of God's promises are fulfilled to perfection and the timing of God's promises are fulfilled with precision. This fact is eloquently stated in another exodus story, *'Now the length of time the Israelite people lived in Egypt was 430 years. At the end of the 430 years, to the very day, all the LORD's divisions left Egypt. Because the LORD kept vigil that night to bring them out of Egypt, on this night all the Israelites are to keep vigil to honour the LORD for the generations to come'* (Ex. 12:40–42). Remarkable isn't it, that God's plan was fulfilled to the very day and we would do well to remember that he is the one who is keeping vigil. His promises and providences are punctual. The eternal purposes of God blossom in due season. There is precision in the fulfilment of prophecy. He will not tire, he will not fall asleep, he will not be distracted or grow disinterested and he will not forget his plans. The events of our lives are not random coincidences; God's clock ticks constantly and strikes true at the correct time.

Our heavenly Father has in his protective care planned good things for us. Jeremiah 29:11 says, *'For I know the plans I have for you,'* declares the LORD, *'plans to prosper you and not to harm you, plans to give you hope and a future.'* Others may have evil intentions towards God's children just as Joseph's brothers had toward him, *'You intended to harm me, but God intended it for good to accomplish what is now being done, the saving of many lives'* (Gen. 50:20). God is directing events towards the conclusion that he desires, so we may echo the words of Paul: *'we know that in all things God works for the good of those who love him, who have been called according to his purpose'* (Rom. 8:28). If we can take hold of this great truth, that the sovereign God is superintending history, we will be spared much anxiety indeed.

One of the many sad chapters in the history of Israel is the seventy-year Babylonian captivity. They had jeered at Jeremiah and contemptuously ignored the repeated warnings of God's servants. They had rebelled and lost their way. Whenever there is such an attitude to the Word of God and contempt for its authority, God's people will inevitably lose their way. By stark contrast we may look at Ezra 6:14, *'So the elders of the Jews continued to build and prosper under the preaching of Haggai the prophet* and *Zechariah, a descendant of Iddo. They finished building the temple according to the command of the God of Israel and the decrees of Cyrus, Darius and Artaxerxes, kings of Persia.'* God has ordained a means by which people may prosper and that is through obedience to the preaching of his Word.

Prophetic preaching

There is a sense in which all preaching is prophetic. The prophets of old were the direct mouthpieces of God and they spoke on his behalf. They predicted events, which had not yet happened and in this sense their preaching was a *foretelling* of the future. But their preaching was also an exposition of the law and in this sense it was a *forth telling* of God's mind. It is in this sense that all preaching has a prophetic dimension, or at least it ought to have. Preaching helps people make sense of their experience and it also helps them to make biblically informed choices. It gives a heavenly perspective on earthly and eternal issues. Often Spirit-anointed preaching will prepare people for future events that the preacher could not have known would happen. It is not that they have extra-biblical knowledge. Rather, through expository preaching a clearer understanding of God's heart, his nature and his work emerges. And frequently this is a Word in season.

The choice of blessing or cursing rests with the hearer of the Word. For those who walk in obedience there is blessing and for those who are wayward there is much grief in store. The people of God found that the geographical distance between Babylon and Jerusalem reflected something of the spiritual distance between themselves and God. They were outside the promises and removed from the blessing. They were estranged from the Lord and under his discipline. What a miserable place to be! The key to blessing is the Word of God; it provides illumination, guidance, counsel and warnings. If we submit to its government we will know blessing, but if we despise its direction the consequences will be catastrophic.

This is what happened to God's people at that time. They had forfeited the blessing and found themselves in bondage. They lost their position of power. Matthew Henry says, 'the crown had fallen from their heads.' They had lost their sense of identity as God's chosen and separate people.

They had lost the freedom to worship. They had shown contempt for that freedom and other privileges and God snatched them away. Perhaps we should look to ourselves and ask if we are indifferent to the great privileges that are ours. In the Western world we take for granted what other believers in many parts of the world would dearly love to have, such as freedom to worship. Are we casual about exercising that freedom? If God were to take it away would we miss it like the people of Israel who remembered better days? In one of the most poignant verses in all of Scripture we read, 'By the rivers of Babylon we sat and wept when we remembered Zion' (Ps. 137:1).

Yet God is faithful, and during the seventy years of captivity he preserved a remnant to return and rebuild. God keeps his promises! This is a thrilling theme that should occupy a central place in our thoughts.

From Babylon to Jerusalem

Ezra begins in Babylon but ends in Jerusalem. It was a new beginning. It was a relatively small beginning in comparison to the great exodus from Egypt under Moses. But it was a beginning in fulfilment of God's Word and they would prosper under the direction of his Word. God had 'stirred up the spirit of Cyrus'. This is all the more remarkable when we consider the fact that Cyrus did not know God. But God knew Cyrus. Matthew Henry says, 'The hearts of Kings are in the hands of the Lord.' Cyrus was a mighty monarch but our God is the mightiest monarch, the King of kings and Lord of lords. He was chosen by God to be instrumental in bringing about the plans of God.

Godless people govern this world but the Lord can influence the spirits of men to do his bidding. He can put thoughts in their minds and give understanding and sympathy where needed. Sound judgement is needed in an amoral and unstable world. The believer is exhorted in Scripture to pray for those in authority (1 Tim. 2:2). We ought to pray that society's laws will reflect Christian morality because even the believer can begin to think that what is legal and what is moral are one and the same when in fact they may be entirely different. Corruption without contrition in high places is rife. People of character are needed to steer the world away from unnecessary conflicts. Political leadership will never deliver the utopia to which it aspires, but good government may create a climate in which the cause of the gospel will prosper, and believers should pray to this end.

Conclusion

God has dates in his diary and his appointments will be kept. Man's plans are subject to frustration. Planes are diverted and delayed. Meetings are deferred and plans are postponed for many and various reasons. But the will of God is on an inexorable course to fulfilment. If God stirs the hearts of those outside his family to do his bidding shouldn't his children be all the more available to work toward the achievement of his aims? Paul charges Timothy to *'stir up the gift of God, which is in thee'* (2 Tim. 1:6 AV). The NIV puts it like this: *'fan into flame the gift of God, which is in you.'* The idea is that the fire has already been kindled but the embers need to be revived. God has deposited his gifts within us and he desires that we use them for his glory. May we find ourselves prospering under the ministry of his Word, by adhering to its efficacious instruction! It is truly amazing grace that he deigns to use us at all.

Questions: for discussion

1. Believers often say, 'God's timing is perfect.' Is that true? Discuss how in principle we understand this truth. (Refer to Ex. 12:40–42 and Gal. 4:4–5). In our practical experience we may sometimes lose sight of that principle. Why?

2. Have you ever experienced God's perfect timing in any situation? Consider this question in the light of God's redeeming purposes in your life and in other areas such as career, marriage etc.

3. Do you believe that God can/does intervene in people's lives today? Examine the following passages of Scripture to determine what light they shed on this. Gen. 50:20 and Acts 17:24–31.

4. To what extent are our spirits stirred within us to grieve at the sight of the sin that surrounds us? Read Acts 17:16–34, how does our attitude to idolatry (in a world that is becoming increasingly pagan and materialistic) compare/contrast with that of the apostle Paul?

5. It is the Holy Spirit who quickens the spirits of men to become conscious of their sinful condition before a holy God. That conviction

of sin may lead to conversion. But the Holy Spirit desires to stir the souls of his people so that their mouths move to speak of Him. How can we create opportunities to share the message of the gospel? How can we take advantage of the opportunities that we already have?

6. What is the meaning of 'prophetic preaching'? What merit does it have for today's church?

The Lord's list

Bible reading: Ezra 2

Focus on...

'Now these are the people of the province who came up from the captivity of the exiles, whom Nebuchadnezzar king of Babylon had taken captive to Babylon (they returned to Jerusalem and Judah, each to his own town ...).' (Ezra 2:1)

Ezra chapter two is a very specific and detailed record of the numbers and occupations of those who returned from Babylon in the first repatriation to Jerusalem under Zerubbabel. It is precisely the kind of passage that we are inclined to skip over in our quiet times and not the kind of chapter one likes to read in public. Considering this it is a good thing that we were not given the responsibility of editing this biblical manuscript for publication. Our tendency would be to omit it altogether as a tedious list of unpronounceable names with very little if any edifying value.

Of course, Ezra is one of the historical books of the *Bible* and as an historical record it is of enormous value. One might be inclined to say that it is important only to the historian, particularly the biblical historian. This would indeed be a poor way of looking at this chapter. Undoubtedly it has historical significance but if we are to believe, as we profess, that it is the Word of God then we must agree that it is profitable to our souls. *'All Scripture is God-breathed and is useful for teaching, rebuking, correcting and training in righteousness, so that the man of God may be thoroughly equipped for every good work'* (2 Tim. 3:16–17). In what way are such passages, and this passage in particular, beneficial to us?

Preserved by the Holy Spirit

The Holy Spirit chose to preserve it as his inspired Word. It is a chronicle that shows us that our God keeps very detailed and specific records. I worked for a couple of years as a tutor in the Irish History Department of University College Cork in Ireland, while I conducted research. This involved consulting various archival records in a number of universities as well as the National Library of Ireland. It introduced me to a lot of primary source documentation which has been subject to diverse interpretations and speculation, particularly in the context of postmodern revisionism which allows for the cultural relativity of truth. While I was a student I worked in the Cork City Museum cataloguing and collating the writings and memorabilia of famous historical personages. My overall impression is that the study of past events in human affairs is sometimes based on sketchy material. I have seen fragments of documents and correspondence with pages missing.

But here is a text, which dates back to the fifth century BC and it preserves the most specific detail. Such a manuscript is a historian's dream and relatively rare. But it is the providential hand of God which has preserved it throughout the centuries and what a marvellous account it is! Perhaps you have tried to trace your ancestry with a view to producing a family tree. Many people who engage in such a project find themselves frustrated by poor parish/church records of marriages, births and deaths. Much more modern records are frequently lost, damaged or destroyed. This comprehensive list is very precise in the detail it records and does not leave room for imaginative speculations. Such minutiae may appear insignificant or irrelevant but the Holy Spirit has been careful to attend to detail. Therefore, this is not trivia, rather it is the Lord's list, which is recorded not only on earth but also in heaven! Rather than seeing this as a tedious catalogue we should see it as a scroll of honour.

Scroll of honour

We live in a world that celebrates achievement by erecting monuments and plaques to commemorate heroic deeds or outstanding merit. Medals and trophies are awarded for athletic prowess and acts of valour. Each community has its scroll of honour and sometimes its heroes are eulogised in song and story. To be remembered is important. Ezra chapter two is something like a scroll of honour. It is, however, a sacred rather than a secular list. God preserved a remnant and each name is a trophy of grace, a testimony to his faithful love and providential care. It demonstrates that his redemptive purposes are still in place and the promised Messiah will come in the fullness of time. These people are not just remembered for posterity, they are remembered for eternity! Their names are known on earth and in heaven. They are not recorded by mistake, as it is God's intention to preserve such a list. The Holy Spirit inspired Ezra to etch these names in eternity. Such a chapter demonstrates the *historicity* of the Bible. Lest we forget it should be stated that we are reading about real people and real events. God said put their names in my book and so it came to pass. He knows them, as he knows all his own, by name.

A remnant preserved by grace

They were a remnant preserved by grace. God has always graciously preserved a remnant unto himself. Thus the apostle Paul says, '*God did not reject his people, whom he foreknew. Don't you know what the Scripture says in the passage about Elijah—how he appealed to God against Israel: "Lord, they have killed your prophets and torn down your altars; I am the only one left, and they are trying to kill me?" And what was God's answer to him? "I have reserved for myself seven thousand who have not bowed the knee to Baal." So too, at the present time there is a remnant chosen by grace. And if by grace, then it is no longer by works; if it were, grace would no longer be grace*' (Rom. 11:2–6).

Whether it is the time of Elijah, the time of the return from Babylonian Captivity, the time at which Paul was writing or today, in every generation God is faithfully preserving a remnant of his grace. And what amazing grace it is! We are saved and sustained by grace. Wretches though we are he quickened our hearts to become conscious of our sin and sinfulness and drew us after him that we might fall at his feet with the burden of an unbearable conviction of sin. It was there that we found unmerited favour in his eyes, for we were helpless and hid ourselves in Christ. Defiled and undeserving he issued a decree that we should be released from bondage and wrote it in his indelible blood. We have been preserved in order that we might be presented before him on that day.

Oh, we may be cynical and say these are the same people who provoked God to punish them (some of them at least). But now they are presented as the remnant of those who have turned their backs on Babylon. They have set their faces toward Jerusalem. They were committed to seeing the honour of God restored and it is through them that the work of God would be revived. It is certain that they are committed to the rebuilding project. May our names be found on such a list of people who are engaged in building for eternity!

A vision for the future

So here we have a list of determined people who believed God and had a vision for the future. They desired to cast off the shackles of captivity and enter the blessing God had prepared. They had come to their senses and would rather be governed by God than by a foreign power and when the opportunity was presented to them they seized it with eagerness. We are presented time and time again with opportunities to turn our backs on the powers that hold us captive. Cyrus was *a* king of kings (an emperor) who was stirred in his spirit by God to issue a decree granting liberty to the captives. Our God is *the* King of kings and from the cross he issued the greatest decree of all when he declared, *'It is finished'*, and lesser powers can have no more dominion.

This is a list of people who desired to rediscover their spiritual identity and forsake that which prevented them from worshipping their God. It was a spiritual dream and they were prepared to work towards seeing it come to fruition. Oh, how we need to give more than lip service to the vision which we have glimpsed and the work to which we say we are ready to be commissioned. Many Christians today are not so much at ease in Zion as they are content in Babylon. These were a people who were discontent in Babylon: *'By the rivers of Babylon we sat and wept when we remembered Zion. There on the poplars we hung our harps, for there our captors asked us for songs, our tormentors demanded songs of joy; they said, "Sing us one of the songs of Zion!" How can we sing the songs of the LORD while in a foreign land? If I forget you, O Jerusalem, may my right hand forget its skill. May my tongue cling to the roof of my mouth if I do not remember you, if I do not consider Jerusalem'* (Ps. 137:1–6).

This is a plaintive song of exile, a mournful remembering of Zion. Their hearts were heavy with sorrow and they wept on the banks of the Tigris and the Euphrates. They longed to be repatriated. Their hearts ached to be restored to a place where they could worship their God. Does anybody long to worship God with this kind of intensity? Such people's names are worth recording!

The sentiment of their hearts may well be seen in the light of the psalm which says, 'As the deer pants for streams of water, so my soul pants for you, O God. My soul thirsts for God, for the living God. When can I go and meet with God? My tears have been my food day and night, while men say to me all day long, "Where is your God?" These things I remember as I pour out my soul...' (Ps. 42:1–4a). He was their heart's desire and they longed to worship him.

Questions: for discussion

1. Do we tend to treat certain passages of God's Word as if they have nothing useful or interesting to say? What does 2 Tim. 3:16 have to teach us?
2. Does such a comprehensive and detailed list reveal anything about the nature and character of God? See Is. 40:26.
3. Is there any sense in which we need to turn our backs on Babylon and be numbered amongst those who are focused on building for eternity?
4. How strong is our desire to worship, work and witness for God?
5. Have we lost that sense that we are engaged in a pioneering project for God? How can we maintain or regain that understanding that we are on the threshold of new frontiers in his work?
6. What does the preservation of this post-exilic remnant of God's people teach us about the Almighty? See Deut. 31:6.

Superficial or sacrificial giving to God

Bible reading: Ezra 2

Focus on ...

'When they arrived at the house of the LORD in Jerusalem, some of the heads of the families gave freewill offerings toward the rebuilding of the house of God on its site. According to their ability they gave to the treasury for this work 61,000 drachmas of gold, 5,000 minas of silver and 100 priestly garments.' (Ezra 2:68–69)

A nother reason why these people are worthy of mention is that they were prepared to give volitionally. Whenever there is sacrificial giving for the work of the Lord there is true heart religion. It is one thing to give in a formal manner out of a sense of obligation or duty but it is another thing entirely to give gladly. There is nothing miserly, half-hearted or begrudging about their giving. They were happy to contribute out of their resources because they had a true sense of the value of spiritual things. It was an outward expression of inner faith. That is what giving to the work of the Lord is: an acknowledgement that all that we have has come from his hand. Those who understand the value of the work of God will give generously. In fact our giving may be measured in proportion to our understanding of this. Somebody has said that our 'giving is measured not by what we give but by what we have left'.

Giving liberally, voluntarily and cheerfully

God's people should always be prepared to give liberally, voluntarily and cheerfully. We may volunteer to give and yet not be very cheerful about it. The Lord was their vision and in the light of that vision everything else paled into insignificance. The apostle Paul stated clearly how God looks on giving: *'Remember this: Whoever sows sparingly will also reap sparingly, and whoever sows generously will also reap generously. Each man should give what he has decided in his heart to give, not reluctantly or under compulsion, for God loves a cheerful giver'* (2 Cor. 9:6–7). We are exhorted to open-handed giving. It is one thing to desire God's work to be done and even to pray fervently to that end but it is another thing to contribute financially to see that vision become a reality. However, a word of caution is needed here, one must pray, pay and play! In other words making a financial contribution may even be a salve to our consciences. In giving we may be excusing ourselves from going and playing our part in the work of God. That would be a bit like the wealthy being exempt from conscription in time of war. That may have been the case in some democracies but it has no place in the divine plan.

Verse sixty-nine of chapter two says that they gave *'according to their ability'*. In the church today some people have substantial resources and others have very little. It is possible, as we all know, for wealthy people to be either generous or mean with what they have. On the other hand we are not so naive as to believe that the less well off are invariably generous by nature. A person of limited means may be generous or have a miserly attitude, although meanness is probably less obvious in the case of the poorer person. It is not right to make a virtue out of either poverty or wealth. The people listed in the second chapter of Ezra gave in proportion to their ability *'to the treasury for this work'* (v. 69). It is the duty of all believers to support the work of the Lord.

The gospels of Luke and Mark draw attention to something important in relation to giving. In their parallel accounts of the 'Widow's Offering' Jesus commended what some might condemn as foolish. We might be inclined to say that unless she develops a more sensible approach to money management she will be trapped in poverty forever. But that is not what God says. Let us look at the passage:

'As he looked up, Jesus saw the rich putting their gifts into the temple treasury. He also saw a poor widow put in two very small copper coins. "I tell you the truth," he said, "this poor widow has put in more than all the others. All these people gave their gifts out of their wealth; but she out of her poverty put in all she had to live on"' (Luke 21:1–4).

Jesus always told the truth, but whenever he uses this phrase, '*I tell you the truth*', as he does here, he is asking his disciples then and now to pay particular attention to the truth being emphasised. What exactly is the truth being underscored here? What Jesus wants us to get hold of is this: there is a vast difference between superficial and sacrificial giving. This widow did not give from a surplus and Jesus commends her for it. There is nothing balanced, or budgeted about her giving. It is not affordable; in fact one could say it appears reckless. But it reflects an attitude of authentic love and depth of faith. There was nothing shallow or partial in the way she gave.

Tokenism dressed up as thanks

Giving must never be tokenism dressed up as thanks. It is a sad fact of life that wealth is a serious obstacle to true spirituality. Whether wealth is amassed through honest or dishonest means one often finds that making money is the chief aim of the wealthy person. It is likely (though not invariably) something to which he has dedicated his life, it has been a single-minded ambition, a number-one priority. Such self-made men are often proud and self-sufficient. They are confident in their own resources and, sadly, arrogant. These people are the chiefs and bosses of their own commercial empires. They find it difficult to be humble and in the church they are sometimes the ones who find it difficult to follow because they are not used to being led. Of course the Holy Spirit can transform such people into what all of us should be, generous to those in need and willing and joyful supporters of the Lord's work. A rich believer can make a very significant contribution to the work of the local church. But even in doing this there is a danger that he sees himself as the paymaster and expects, by virtue of that to call the shots. The 'he who pays the piper calls the tune' attitude has no place in the church of Christ. It should be remembered that God does not need our money to accomplish his purposes. Rather, he desires our cheerful willingness to give sacrificially rather than superficially. This is not a Marxist analysis of economics; rather, it is a biblical perspective which needs to be preached without fear or favour.

It has been my experience that wealthy people don't give like poor people. I have heard those who can afford to contribute to a particular situation say things like, 'I don't want to encourage idleness,' or 'I would not like to create false expectations.' They are prepared to argue that money won't make any real difference and what is really required is better financial management and budgeting skills. On the face of it their reasoning seems to be sensible because there is a good deal of truth in what they say. However, my experience is that poorer people just give. It is not that they are unaware of these arguments, even if they are articulated less eloquently. They are generally more compassionate than critical. Now I'm not saying that all those who have wealth lack compassion because that would simply be untrue, unfair and unkind, but generally, those who value money more than anything else are reluctant to part with it. We can rationalise our rationing but God expects us to give generously. Many a Christian's wallet or purse is unconverted! They are saved but their pockets are sown up. Jesus observed what people were giving and he still does that. He sees the motives and the excuses.

God is generous

One very good reason for showing generosity is that God is himself generous by nature. If we desire to be truly like him then we should not neglect to be generous. That generosity is most evident in his willingness to forgive our great debt of sin. The ledger has been balanced because he paid the price in full. Luke records the thinking of Jesus on this issue, *'Give, and it will be given to you. A good measure, pressed down, shaken together and running over, will be poured into your lap. For with the measure you use, it will be measured to you'* (Luke 6:38). I remember often as a child being sent to the local shop to buy cheese. The shopkeeper would cut the required amount from an enormous slab and weigh it on the scales. He was very particular and never exceeded the weight. However, when his wife served me my mother always knew because she gave a good measure. Recently my wife returned from the supermarket and I was helping to store the groceries. I took the bag of sugar and filled the sugar bowl. When it appeared full I gave the bowl a couple of shakes and the volume settled down allowing more space in the bowl so I added more sugar. I had almost emptied the bag so I pressed the sugar down in the bowl with a spoon and emptied the remaining contents into the bowl. I estimated incorrectly and it overflowed making quite a mess. I was summarily banished from the kitchen but on reflection that is what Jesus said God's generosity is like. He pours a quart into a pint pot. Paul prays that the Ephesians *'may be filled to the measure of all the fullness of God'* (Eph. 3:19).

The rich young man that had done everything required in the law was unwilling to sell all that he had and give it to the poor as Jesus suggested. Ultimately money meant more to him than obeying the master. Jesus could read his heart and knew how to touch the central issue. I have heard it said that many of us would not be prepared to follow Jesus on those terms in a way that suggests that Jesus was unreasonable in his demands on this young man. Unless we are prepared to do that we need not count ourselves as disciples of Jesus at all.

May our names be listed in heaven with those who turned their backs on Babylon. May we be identified with those who are bound for Zion. May we be listed with those who give sacrificially to the work of God. May we reflect something of the generosity of his true nature.

Questions: for discussion

1. How would you explain the difference between superficial and sacrificial to the work of the Lord?
2. What should be our attitude in giving to the work of the Lord? See 2 Cor. 9:6–7; Luke 6:38; 1 Tim. 6:17–19.
3. Not everybody is called to enter fulltime service for God but is it possible that giving financially to the work of God is sometimes a salve to the consciences of those who are not willing to go into that work when prompted by God?
4. Is there anything in the character and nature of God that should inspire us to give liberally? See Eph. 2:8–9 and Matt. 20:1–16 (note v. 15).
5. Some might be inclined to think that Jesus was too harsh with the rich young man (see Matt.19:16–30). What do you understand as the implications for discipleship from this passage, especially in relation to those who possess wealth?
6. In the passage that we know as 'The Widow's Offering' (Luke 21:1–4) Jesus observes the giving of rich and poor alike. He commends the

widow for contributing 'all she had to live on' whereas we might be inclined to criticise such behaviour as reckless. How does this challenge us in today's church?

Undivided urgency

Bible reading: Ezra 3

Focus on...

'...the people assembled as one man in Jerusalem.' (Ezra 3:1)

The Feast of Booths

It was the seventh month, the month of Tishri, when the people assembled in unison for the Feast of Tabernacles which was also known as the Feast of Booths or the Feast of In-gathering. The modern calendar equivalent to the month of Tishri would be September/October. It was a seven-day event celebrated from the fifteenth day to the twenty-first day, inclusive. During this period fruit was gathered and people lived in booths made of branches of trees.

This was a biblical[1] Jewish feast. Thus we read in Exodus, 'Celebrate the Feast of Ingathering at the end of the year, when you gather in your crops from the field...' (Ex. 23:16). In Numbers we read, 'On the fifteenth day of the seventh month, hold a sacred assembly and do no regular work. Celebrate a festival to the LORD for seven days' (Num. 29:12). Detailed instruction is given about how the feast is to be celebrated and what offerings are to be made each day. Also in Leviticus we read, '"So beginning with the fifteenth day of the seventh month, after you have gathered the crops of the land, celebrate the festival to the LORD for seven days; the first day is a day of rest, and the eighth day also is a day of rest. On the first day you are to take choice fruit from the trees, and palm fronds, leafy branches and poplars, and rejoice before the LORD your God for seven days. Celebrate this as a festival to the LORD for seven days each year. This is to be a lasting ordinance for the generations to come; celebrate it in the seventh month. Live in booths for seven days: All native-born Israelites are to live in booths so your descendants will know that I had the Israelites live in booths when I brought them out of

Egypt. I am the LORD your God." So Moses announced to the Israelites the appointed feasts of the LORD' (Lev. 23:39–44).

We learn from Nehemiah that the people rediscovered, from Scripture, their privileged responsibility to engage in the celebration of the Feast of Booths: *'On the second day of the month, the heads of all the families, along with the priests and the Levites, gathered around Ezra the scribe to give attention to the words of the Law. They found written in the Law, which the LORD had commanded through Moses, that the Israelites were to live in booths during the feast of the seventh month and that they should proclaim this word and spread it throughout their towns and in Jerusalem: "Go out into the hill country and bring back branches from olive and wild olive trees, and from myrtles, palms and shade trees, to make booths"—as it is written. So the people went out and brought back branches and built themselves booths on their own roofs, in their courtyards, in the courts of the house of God and in the square by the Water Gate and the one by the Gate of Ephraim. The whole company that had returned from exile built booths and lived in them. From the days of Joshua son of Nun until that day, the Israelites had not celebrated it like this. And their joy was very great'* (Neh. 8:13–17).

A range of emotions

The first day was to be a holy convocation and the day after the feast they were to hold an assembly and do no regular work (Num. 29:35). Although the people would have been summoned to assemble this was not merely a formal convening of a people who reluctantly or begrudgingly gathered together. The feasts were meant to be occasions of heartfelt joy and great celebration. So at the opening of chapter three we encounter the people of God meeting together in Jerusalem. It is very difficult to imagine how they felt. They had been captives in Babylon where they did not have the freedom to worship. Nebuchadnezzar of Babylon had captured Jerusalem in 597 BC and ten years later destroyed the city and its Temple. The great and ancient city lay in ruins and the remnant of God's people now stood in the rubble. It must have been a humbling experience.

They had sat by the Tigris and Euphrates and wept when they considered the privileges they had scorned and forfeited. They had taken the opportunity to return under the leadership of Zerubbabel and contributed to the cost of rebuilding voluntarily. Now they were in Jerusalem, the spiritual capital of their true homeland. It is not easy for us to appreciate the depth of feeling they experienced at that time. As they stood in the ruined city they must have been conscious that they were on the site where they had offended God by their disobedience and infidelity. Yet it was the very place where God had chosen to manifest his presence and glory. They had provoked God to punish them and now there was a new beginning, a glorious opportunity to start over again.

It is reasonable to assume that they experienced a range of emotions. There must have been an overwhelming sense of relief that they had actually arrived. There were probably feelings of remorse that they had ever got themselves into a situation whereby they were led captive in the first place. Perhaps they had left friends and even family in Babylon and their hearts were grieving for them. Maybe there was a sense of elation at this new liberty. Were they discouraged by the scale of the project before them? Did the sight of the old temple in ruins sadden them?

Surely it was a daunting task that lay ahead. But we read that '...*the people assembled as one man in Jerusalem'*, which indicates not only a sense of unity, but also a sense of urgency. They were united by one urgent purpose, to engage in the rebuilding project. They were focused on the achievement of this vision. There were no absentees and of those who assembled there was no apathy. There was nothing casual or routine about this gathering. Here were a people who met with determination and resolve. They were committed to the work of the Lord and they assembled with expectant hearts. They were people who had ministered in the Temple as servants and singers and gatekeepers and priests. They assembled now to be commissioned. God was about to direct them and they were ready to do his bidding.

Here are a people sifted and refined by the calamity that had befallen them and now they realised that the task, which lay ahead, would require a united effort. So this chapter begins by showing that service to God requires united effort.

Service demands obedience

Then the second verse of chapter three shows that service to God requires leadership and obedience to his Word: *'Then Jeshua son of Jozadak and his fellow priests and Zerubbabel son of Shealtiel and his associates began to build the altar of the God of Israel to sacrifice burnt offerings on it, in accordance with what is written in the Law of Moses the man of God.'* Those in leadership began the work of building an altar so that the people could once again worship God in the manner appointed in the law. The people were not driven; they were led and they willingly followed. There was supervision of the work. Verse nine tells us that Jeshua and others *'joined together in supervising those working on the house of God.'* The leadership may delegate the work of God but it certainly needs supervision. It is not the supervision of taskmasters but the support and oversight of those whom God has appointed to protect and promote the work.

A word on worship

We must always worship God by adhering to the principles that he has given to us in his precious Word. It is not for us to invent new ways of approaching him. The first question in determining the manner of our worship must always be what does he require of us? It should be our desire to please him. This is particularly true of those in positions of leadership who should be conscious that obedience to the Word of God is expected always. Scripture is to be the rule in all matters of faith and practice. It is the only authority in guiding belief and behaviour. There is an attitude in today's church that worship is something for us. It is wonderful to sense the presence of God in our times of worship and it truly warms our hearts but we ought not to come to God with a 'what can I get out of this time of worship?' attitude. Worship is about giving to God and only when we do that will we sense the nearness of his beloved presence.

Courage in the face of opposition

Let us look at the next verse: *'Despite their fear of the peoples around them, they built the altar on its foundation and sacrificed burnt offerings on it to the LORD, both the morning and evening sacrifices'* (v. 3). The work of the Lord requires courage in the face of opposition. Today, as then, God's people are surrounded by those who see them as crackpots, narrow-minded bigots, moralistic killjoys and cranks. We are not being paranoid. Derision and ridicule will attend those who engage wholeheartedly in God's work. Our hearts may be fearful but our focus should be on God's work.

Christ the cornerstone

The foundation for our work is Calvary. There is no other altar. Jesus has been sacrificed once for all who trust in his shed blood. Our worship is to be built on the foundation of the cross. We are to celebrate that act of redemptive love and eternal justice as foundational in our faith. Ours is a table of remembrance rather than an altar. We look back at what has already been accomplished by the shedding of the precious blood of our Saviour. We look into our hearts to ensure that there is no sin harbouring there. We look up to heaven where Jesus is seated at the right hand side of the Father and makes intercession for us. And we look forward to his return because we take the emblems of his death, the bread and the cup, until he comes. They are symbols, no more and no less, and how appropriate they are when we think that the grain from which we get bread and the grape from which we get wine both go through a process of crushing. He was crushed for our iniquities and we remember our sin with sorrow and our salvation with the joy of forgiveness. It is a reverent celebration. The only altar we build is a biblical understanding of the cross, which is the foundational theology of our worship. He is the cornerstone of the church. *'The church's one foundation is Jesus Christ our Lord.'*

Complacency and the cross

Verse three says that they *'sacrificed burnt offerings on it to the LORD, both the morning and evening sacrifices.'* It is a sad fact of life that many churches, which once met twice on the Lord's day, have decided to cancel their evening services. Indeed it could be said that for many the concept of the Lord's day has been replaced by the idea of the Lord's half-day. It could be argued that meeting twice on Sunday is merely a cultural practice and that allowing it to fall into abeyance is not sinful. That may indeed be true, but is it not a sad reflection on the level of our commitment that we give so little of our time to him? A glorious opportunity is lost to an entire generation. Perhaps we should remove that chorus from our hymnals which says, *'From the rising of the sun to the going down of the same, the Lord's name is to be praised.'* For these people who were fresh out of Babylon they saw it as a great privilege to engage in communal worship at the beginning and the end of the day. When the sense of the greatness of that redemption and the opportunity it affords begins to wear off we take for granted a great privilege and then we contemptuously cast it aside. How terribly sad! Can you imagine the persecuted church, where meeting together involves risking liberty or life itself, spurning such opportunity? May God help us to overcome our complacency and avail ourselves of the privileges and opportunities that are ours.

Division of labour

In verse seven we read, *'Then they gave money to the masons and carpenters...'* This shows us that when the building of the temple got underway there was a division of labour. In the great project facing the church today there must also be opportunity for those who have gifts and talents to bring those into the service of the Lord. May those with such gifts and talents be challenged to make them available for the building up of his church? We are, after all, *'Facing a task unfinished.'* We need to cast off our complacency and love of ease and commit the work to the Lord in prayer. There are still forces that defy the work of God. The surrounding people are crying out in despair, disillusioned with false religion and politics. We are a commissioned people who bear the torch of the gospel in this dark world. The message of salvation is unchanged and the power of God is unchanged. What has changed is our commitment and ambition to see the cause of the gospel succeed! Many withhold their abilities from the service of Christ's church or they give so much and say, 'I have given enough.' Say it if you will, but those words are heard in heaven and on earth. It must grieve God who gave his only begotten Son to hear Christians say, 'I've done my bit'. May God stir up fervency within us that burns brightly, may he sustain us when we are tired! Oh, we may become tired *in* the work but may we never become tired *of* the work! May God preserve us from the fear that sometimes inhibits us!

Questions: for discussion

1. What do you think was the likely attitude of heart of the people of

God as they assembled for the feast of Booths for the first time since the seventy-year Babylonian captivity?

2. What do you understand by the statement '...*the people assembled as one man in Jerusalem*' (Ezra 3:1)?

3. Is there any sense in which we need to rediscover our privileged responsibilities? See 1 Pet. 2:4–10 and Heb. 4:14–16.

4. Are our times of public worship characterised by unity and urgency? What do absenteeism and apathy in churches today tell us about attitudes to God?

5. In the light of the cross how do you see Christian commitment and complacency?

6. Consider the division of labour within your own church and discuss where people fit in to that structure.

Footnote

1 Some feasts were extra-biblical.

Lamenting or lauding labour for the Lord?

Bible reading: Ezra 3

Focus on...

'When the builders laid the foundation of the temple of the LORD, the priests in their vestments and with trumpets, and the Levites (the sons of Asaph) with cymbals, took their places to praise the LORD, as prescribed by David king of Israel. With praise and thanksgiving they sang to the LORD: "He is good; his love to Israel endures for ever." And all the people gave a great shout of praise to the LORD, because the foundation of the house of the LORD was laid. But many of the older priests and Levites and family heads, who had seen the former temple, wept aloud when they saw the foundation of this temple being laid, while many others shouted for joy. No one could distinguish the sound of the shouts of joy from the sound of weeping, because the people made so much noise. And the sound was heard far away.' (Ezra 3:10–13)

Here is one of the most poignant moments in Scripture. It is a deeply moving scene that arouses our sympathy. The builders had laid the foundation of the temple of the Lord (v. 10). Then the people gathered in an organised manner 'as prescribed by David king of Israel' (v. 10). They sang about the goodness of God, the love of God, his covenant relationship to his chosen people and his faithfulness. Perhaps this is the keynote refrain of their glorious theme and not merely a repetitive phrase chanted repeatedly like a trance inducing mantra as happens in some religious traditions. It may well be the title of a great hymn of praise and it certainly bears a remarkable resemblance to Psalms 107 and 136.[1]

Their singing was accompanied by the sound of trumpets and cymbals. The most appropriate word that comes to mind to describe the 'music' is *loud*. I do not think we are meant to infer from this that loud music is appropriate in worship, that somehow volume captures the sense of triumph. It is wonderful to hear good congregational singing and there is nothing wrong with loud singing. It is worth mentioning that the Primitive Methodists were known for their loud singing which offended the traditionalists! It is not the volume of our singing that causes it to be heard in heaven. Rather it is the sincerity of heart confessing great truths prayerfully in song that ascends to the throne of the Lamb as sweet incense. Here in Ezra this was essentially a declaration to themselves and an announcement to the surrounding peoples that they had accomplished the first significant objective in their aim to re-establish temple worship. If it is a liturgical response then it is certainly sung with depth of feeling for we read that many *'wept aloud'* and others *'shouted for joy'*. There is nothing parrot-like in it. This is not merely a formal ceremonial event where the congregation repeats a well-rehearsed phrase on cue. Neither is it only a spontaneous overflow of feeling where the people's emotions are stirred to frenzy. Although there is great depth of feeling expressed, it is nevertheless an organised occasion where people *'took their places to praise the Lord, as prescribed…'* (v. 10), and the moment was such that it elicited authentic heart-felt response from the people.

Lamentation and Celebration

It is a vivid and animated picture of the moment. There is a mingling of emotions. The lamentation of the old and the celebration of the young are juxtaposed and what heart could not be moved to pity with such a picture? There is a note of triumph, a note of sorrow and a note of joy in the occasion.

Surely it is like our gathering at the Lord's Table. Our time of communion is a time for singing songs of victory and it is a time of sorrow that leads to repentance. Yet it is an occasion to be celebrated. Perhaps we celebrate with less noise (depending on our culture and traditions) but may it never be with less affection for the glory of God, less consciousness of his covenant relationship to his people, less awareness of his goodness and love or with diminished understanding of his faithfulness. Partaking of the emblems of bread and wine ought to elicit both sorrow and joy as we contemplate the fact that he laid down his life to be the foundation of the church. Each stone put in place is marked with his precious blood.

The master mason is at work

I remember many years ago visiting the lovely English town of Cambridge. It is, of course, a place of great history and the university dominates everything else. When I was walking through one of the several campuses I saw masons at work. They were rebuilding a section of wall that had been demolished for some reason. I noticed that a number clearly written in red paint marked each stone. Obviously each stone had a correct place in the structure. It reminds me of Christ the master mason of the church. He has marked every believer with his precious blood and is fitting each one into place.

He is building his church and no opposition will thwart its completion. He is supervising the work along with those whom he has appointed to oversee it. We read in verse eight that *'all who had returned from captivity to Jerusalem began the work.'* Each one was commissioned, nobody was redundant by virtue of age, gender or any other consideration. It was a joint endeavour of willing workers, which the Lord was pleased to bless.

The leaders were focused on the spiritual welfare of the people and this is shown in the way that they led the rebuilding of the altar so that the people may engage in worship. The fact that they prioritised this project shows a real awareness of their understanding of the importance of worship. The altar and worship had been neglected in the past and the result was that they became contaminated by the idolatrous practices of the surrounding peoples. In order to prevent any repetition of past failures they hastened to prioritise the building of the altar.

The first step in idolatry

When people neglect to worship God in the manner prescribed and in the freedom afforded and allow such opportunities to go unobserved it is the first step on the route that ultimately leads to idolatry. When we give that time and place to other things or people instead of God we are failing to honour him as he desires and demands. The lesson had been learned very deeply for the people never again returned to idolatry. But it was a lesson learned at great cost. If only we would listen to God and spare ourselves, by so doing, the great troubles we bring upon our lives.

The myth of nostalgia

There is a word of caution to be gleaned from the verses under consideration. It is wonderful to look back over the past and remember with joy the faithfulness of God and to celebrate that. Surely we can say *'thus far has the Lord helped us.'* We can give testimony to the reality of his grace and its sufficiency in all situations. He has supplied all our needs and all the honour and glory is due to him. However, when looking back makes us discontented to such an extent that we discount present spiritual activity as worthy of celebration then we are despising the work of God. In lands that have been privileged to know great revivals, the saints of succeeding generations may tend to mythologise the past. Oh, it is right to desire to see God move in our generation in mighty power. Was that not the prayer of Habakkuk? *'LORD, I have heard of your fame; I stand in awe of your deeds, O LORD. Renew them in our day, in our time make them known; in wrath remember mercy'* (Hab. 3:2). But if our nostalgic view of the past paralyses work in the present, then it is nothing more than a good appreciation of God's previous work serving a bad purpose. We are not to sit idly waiting for revival, rather we are to hoist our sails and do all within our means so that when the wind blows it will catch the sail and carry the vessel along and even then it must be steered in a purposeful course. We cannot conjure up revival but we can at least work toward creating the favourable conditions in which God deigns to work.

Which one of us can look back and not feel a tinge of regret that there were times when we neglected to worship and serve our precious Saviour as we should? Times when we failed him. Consciousness of our own great weakness may bring tears to our eyes but those tears should not blind us to the reality of his presence and power. If they had known that one day the Messiah would enter the synagogue at Nazareth and take the scroll and read: *'The Spirit of the Lord is on me, because he has anointed me to preach good news to the poor. He has sent me to proclaim freedom for the prisoners and recovery of sight for the blind, to release the oppressed, to proclaim the year of the Lord's favour'* (Luke 4:18–19); if they had any inclination that the incarnate God almighty would stand in a building constructed by their descendants and declare his identity and intentions when he said: *'Today this Scripture is fulfilled in your hearing'* (Luke 4:20), then they may have been more forward looking in both their approach to the work and their appreciation of it. May the Lord inhabit the work of our hands as we build for eternity.

Questions: for discussion

1. True worship engages our emotional and mental faculties and must be conducted decently, in an orderly manner and in accordance with the prescribed principles of Scripture? Why? What does Ezra 3:10–13 reveal to us about this issue?
2. Why is the Lord's Table a time of happiness and heartache? See 1 Pet. 1:8–21.
3. How do God's people begin the journey into idolatry?
4. Considering that some people tend to idealise the past while others dismiss it as old-fashioned and irrelevant, is nostalgia, therefore, a bane or blessing?
5. There is a relationship between our appreciation of the Lord's work and our approach to it. How does an eternal perspective (rather than a temporal perspective) assist worship, stimulate holiness and inform and motivate evangelism?
6. Although worship is primarily adoration of God for who he is and for his redemptive work at Calvary, there is also an evangelistic dimension to our public worship. How can we give due and proportionate emphasis to this evangelistic dimension without compromising what God desires and deserves from us?

Footnote

1 I'm not suggesting that a chorus should be repeated twenty six times to match the refrain of Psalm 136!

Union, uniformity or unity?

Bible reading: Ezra 3

Focus on…

'… the people assembled as one man in Jerusalem' (Ezra 3:1).

The first group of exiles had returned from captivity in Babylon to begin rebuilding the altar and re-establishing temple worship. It was an important occasion in the life of the people. There was neither absenteeism nor apathy.

One might be tempted to suggest that because they were a homogeneous ethnic group they were more likely to experience unity. Consider, however, how even small families can have diverse interests and the level of energy expended by parents in seeking to harmonise activity to suit all parties, and you soon appreciate the divine nature of unity! It is difficult to achieve consensus even with a few people.

The organic nature of unity

What does it mean to assemble 'as one man'? A man has one head, a rather obvious point one might say! Let us not overlook the obvious. One man has one mind to govern and guide him. Christ is the head of the church and the mind of the majority must harmonise with the mind of the Master. An individual has one heart that harbours his hopes. One man has certain appetites and aspirations. When a man feels hungry his body craves food, when he is thirsty he desires to quench that thirst. When a man feels tired he longs for rest or recreation. One man feels pleasure or pain in any given part of the body. There is one nervous system. One man has singular vision and perspective. He is single-minded in his dedication to the achievement of his aims.

The words '…*the people assembled as one man in Jerusalem*' identify an organic unity that existed between them. It is not merely that they were united by a common purpose, although that was their focus, they were also united in a covenant relationship to God and to each other. Just as the human body is a complex organism of diverse parts functioning together as a whole, so too was this assembly. The unity of the body is physiological and psychological. This key verse draws attention to the fact that there was an organic spiritual unity amongst the children of God. It was not merely an organisational harmony or an artificial, imposed order. On the contrary, it was a natural thing.

A picture of how we are to be in Christ

Here were a people who were united and of one accord and it is a picture of how we are to be in Christ. Paul tells the Romans that *'in Christ we who are many form one body, and each member belongs to all the others'* (Rom. 12:5). We know that divisions weaken the church. This problem is well illustrated in the Corinthian church where there was jealousy, quarrelling and worldliness: *'You are still worldly. For since there is jealousy and quarrelling among you, are you not worldly?'* (1 Cor. 3:3). Paul entreated them to work toward agreement, *'I appeal to you, brothers, in the name of our Lord Jesus Christ, that all of you agree with one another so that there may be no divisions among you and that you may be perfectly united in mind and thought'* (1 Cor. 1:10).

Unity is to be the aim of all Christians. Jesus prayed for it: *'I pray also for those who will believe in me through their message, that all of them may be one, Father, just as you are in me and I am in you'* (John 17:20–21). Paul understood that God had given certain gifts to the church *'so that the body of Christ may be built up until we all reach unity in the faith and in the knowledge of the Son of God and become mature, attaining to the whole measure of the fullness of Christ'* (Eph. 4:12b-13). If Jesus prayed for it and Paul pleaded for it and preached about it then we must practise it!

What is unity?

It is important to clarify what we mean when we talk about unity. Firstly, unity is not uniformity. Scripture teaches that there is unity in diversity. There is no contradiction here, as Paul explains to the Romans, *'Just as each of us has one body with many members, and these members do not all have the same function, so in Christ we who are many form one body, and each member belongs to all the others. We have different gifts, according to the grace given us.'* (Rom. 12:4–6). So there is variety of function with overall unity. Secondly, unity is not 'union'. In marriage, for example, there may be union without unity. In such a marriage there is discord rather than harmony and yet it is a legal union. Unity and union are different. Union artificially binds together dissimilar elements whereas Christian unity is an outworking of the inner work of the Holy Spirit.

We read in Ephesians, *'As a prisoner for the Lord, then, I urge you to live a life worthy of the calling you have received. Be completely humble and gentle; be patient, bearing with one another in love. Make every effort to keep the unity of the Spirit through the bond of peace. There is one body and one Spirit...'* (Eph. 4:1–3). Here Paul is encouraging the believers at Ephesus to maintain a unity that already exists and is based upon the foundational truths he has outlined in the previous three chapters. So it is a unity which is maintained by humility, gentleness, patience and love. The other side of that same coin is that it is damaged or destroyed by pride, arrogance (often dressed up as assertiveness), impatience and anything that falls short of love.

In the first three chapters of Ephesians Paul has been speaking about being made alive in Christ and the spiritual blessings that are in Christ. So when he says, *'then, I urge you'*, we ought to pay particular attention to the word *'then'* or as the AV puts it *'therefore'*. We are not being pedantic in doing this; we are merely following the sense of the message. Someone once said when you see a *'therefore'* in Scripture you should ask 'what is it *there for'*? Paul is actually saying, 'In the light of all the great doctrines I have been outlining, maintain the unity that is based on these great truths.' We cannot divorce the two and we should not want to separate them.

The emphasis in chapter one of Ephesians is that God desires unity but sin obstructs and divides. We experience the inward struggle between good and evil and the outward struggle between man and man. Thus the world has been damaged by sin but the aim of regeneration is to reverse that process of degeneration. God's redemptive plan is essentially about reconciliation between God and man. In reuniting man with himself God is restoring the fellowship and unity that existed before the fall. When man sinned there was a severing of that relationship. Thus chapter two of Ephesians speaks about the middle wall of partition (between God and the regenerate) being broken down. Then chapter three goes on to talk about the unity of Jew and Gentile in Christ. We must note that such unity exists *'in Christ'* and that no such unity exists outside Christ! Thus when Paul comes to chapter four he stresses the importance of maintaining that unity by being vigilant about our attitudes and actions. The Christian church as the body of Christ is to reflect the unity that exists in the Godhead. It is a unity of truth and love.

Paul is not merely urging the church at Ephesus to develop a sense of camaraderie. He talks of *'the unity of the Spirit'* and we must note that it is the Holy Spirit that is referred to here. It is a unity created by the work of the Holy Spirit in regeneration. It is impossible for us to create this unity. But all that are thus united are asked to work towards its maintenance. Therefore, it is our duty to maintain unity based on truth and to ignore calls for associations and amalgamations masquerading as unity, however eloquent they may be.

Questions: for discussion

1. How is unity organic in nature? See Rom. 12:4–6; Eph. 1:22–23 and discuss how these Scriptures assume a unity among believers based on our unity *'in Christ'*.
2. What is our role in maintaining this unity? See Eph. 4:1–3; 1 Cor. 1:10; Phil. 2:1–5.
3. What is the difference between unity and union?
4. What is the difference between unity and uniformity? See Rom. 12:4–6 and Gal. 3:28.
5. 2 Cor. 1:7 speaks of sharing both sufferings and comfort. How is this a practical expression of Christian unity?
6. Consider Gal. 5:16–26. In this passage the works of the flesh and the fruit of the Holy Spirit are contrasted. Consider the nine fruits of the Spirit and explain how they each contribute to maintaining unity in the local church.

Discerning danger in proposals for partnership

Bible reading: Ezra 4

Focus on...

'When the enemies of Judah and Benjamin heard that the exiles were building a temple for the LORD, the God of Israel, they came to Zerubbabel and to the heads of the families and said, "Let us help you build because, like you, we seek your God and have been sacrificing to him since the time of Esarhaddon king of Assyria, who brought us here." But Zerubbabel, Jeshua and the rest of the heads of the families of Israel answered, "You have no part with us in building a temple to our God. We alone will build it for the LORD, the God of Israel, as King Cyrus, the king of Persia, commanded us."' (Ezra 4:1–3)

The need for clarity today

Perhaps this statement from the leaders that they would not accept the offer of help extended to them seems discourteous. But there is no evidence here to indicate that they erred, and to suggest that they did would be a completely unwarranted inference imposed on the Scriptures. On the contrary, they were the ones who were commissioned in this work of construction and they are quite clear about whom they should work with and whom they should not work with. The people who requested that they be allowed to be involved were from Samaria. After the fall of Samaria (721–722 BC) Mesopotamians and Arameans settled in the area. They worshipped their own gods but also took up the worship of the Lord as the god of the land. This kind of syncretism was and still is sacrilegious and any partnership with such people can only dilute the identity of God's people.

Such clarity is needed today! It is the responsibility of those who are in covenant relationship with God to carry on the work of construction. It is not appropriate to form unholy alliances. Our partnership in the work of God must be with those who are chosen, converted and commissioned to this work.

A danger discerned and decisive action

Chapter four of Ezra is an account of the opposition of some people to the work of rebuilding the temple. The leaders immediately recognised that the offer of help from those who were not in covenant relationship with the God of Israel would compromise the integrity of the work. They were not prepared to see the people of God working side by side with people outside that covenant. This work of construction was a project that was intended to be to the glory of God. The kind of interaction that would inevitably have resulted from accepting the offer of help would have compromised the integrity of that work. Whether it is wielding the sword or the trowel for God we must be careful not to engage in inappropriate alliances.

The leaders and the people could have said, 'We could do with help, it is a daunting task, they have offered their skills and talents to this work and it would be rude and offensive to decline to accept.' They could have said, 'Let them work alongside us and we will influence them in the hope that they may come to worship our God too.' But the leadership realised that this would not be the likely outcome. Rather, accepting the offer of help would undermine the work by forging relationships that would potentially distort the true spiritual perspective and practices of God's people.

Not dithering about where we stand

There were no dissenting voices to this decision and this is evidence of the harmonious understanding that existed between them all. Such unity is to be highly prized indeed. There would have been real problems in the future if such a partnership had been forged. The co–opted group would not only have influenced the workers but they would probably have asserted their right to involvement in the temple worship itself. After all if their labour were acceptable then they would have some basis to further claims. The leaders were right, therefore, to recognise that the offer of co-operation would in fact be a form of opposition to the work.

The unregenerate are enemies of God and it is unwise and dangerous to develop links with God's enemies to do God's work. Our relationship with the world is one of witnessing for Christ in the work of the gospel. Forging unhelpful and unhealthy alliances that contribute to creating the impression of unity where none exists undermines this. Some may be tempted to work with those who speak a similar language to achieve certain objectives. This policy is often referred to as 'co-belligerency'. The idea goes something like this: the Roman Catholic Church is opposed to abortion and the evangelical Christian is also opposed to non-therapeutic abortion so why not get together to fight against abortion on demand. In this way believers may be attracted to establish temporary relationships with non-believers so that they can pool their resources, plan campaigns and promote the greater social good. But what we must bear in mind is the fact that this is not merely social work in the same way as the rebuilding of the temple was not merely physical work. The construction of the temple was a spiritual process toward a spiritual product and as such it could not really be solved in purely manpower terms.

The problem of poor principles

When a church needs extra helpers in any area of its life it must not look to its unconverted adherents to conduct that work. One might ask 'what harm is there in engaging somebody to do a work that is not really 'spiritual' such as supervising the toddlers and babies in the crèche?' The argument might go something like this: 'working in the crèche is not a spiritual work like teaching in Sunday school.' The argument may be subtle and even persuasive but there is peril in adopting such principles. Zerubbabel could have said, 'Well, seeing as you will be only mixing mortar and digging the foundation and hauling rubble away and seeing as it is only carpentry and masonry and so on I suppose we could use you.' But he didn't!

This great enterprise that we are engaged in, every facet of it is God's work. The leadership was not deceived. They detected the danger inherent in the offer and rejected it unequivocally. It was a wise and godly decision determined not on the basis of reason alone but on the basis of reason informed by wisdom from on high. *'But Zerubbabel, Jeshua and the rest of the heads of the families of Israel answered, "You have no part with us in building a temple to our God. We alone will build it for the LORD, the God of Israel..."'* (4:3). It was not an unfortunate reaction but a response of faith.

The same principle that informed their decision must permeate our thinking. God must be our God if we are to engage in a spiritual enterprise for him. It is wrong to work in partnership with those who are not in covenant relationship with him as it is an offence to God. Moreover, it is doing a great disservice to the unconverted by conveying a false sense of security. It is cruel to create a sense of belonging to the family of God when in fact they do not belong to him.

Paul put it plainly to a people who had a proclivity to forming improper partnerships, *'Do not be yoked together with unbelievers. For what do righteousness and wickedness have in common? Or what fellowship can light have with darkness? What harmony is there between Christ and Belial? What does a believer have in common with an unbeliever? What agreement is there between the temple of God and idols? For we are the temple of the living God. As God has said: "I will live with them and walk among them, and I will be their God, and they will be my people." Therefore, "Come out from them and be separate, says the Lord. Touch no unclean thing, and I will receive you"'* (2 Cor. 6:14–17). These words need to be preached in a pluralist society where evangelical Christianity is being drawn into the ecumenical vortex. It is only by adhering to his precepts that we appropriate his promises in our lives.

Many people are deceived in believing that their religious service to God merits his favour. We must be careful not to create such false hope. Jesus will one day reject many people who have assumed that they belong to him. He will say, *'I never knew you. Away from me, you evildoers!'* (Matt. 7:23). They will cite in their own defence the work they have undertaken in the kingdom but God will accept only those who are his by virtue of the new covenant.

Questions: for discussion

1. These *'enemies of Judah'* worshipped their own gods but also took up the worship of the Lord as the god of the land. What does God think of that sort of 'worship'? See Ex. 20:2–6 and Acts 17:16–34.

2. There are healthy and holy partnerships as well as unhealthy and unhelpful ones. What can we learn from the following Scriptures concerning this matter? Phil. 1:3–6; 2 Cor. 6:14–17.

3. One of the dangers in forging unnatural partnerships with individuals or organisations is a dilution of the message of the gospel. Consider the implications of this for today's church.

4. How can we be more discerning in a world where there are many pressures to conform to the expectations of those who desire partnerships by trivialising truth? See James 1:5.

5. In a world that reveres tolerance as the supreme virtue and reviles those who reject the pluralist agenda how can the evangelical Christian communicate his faith without compromising? See Eph. 4:11–16 and note verse 15.

6. In recent years some Christian agencies have gone outside the evangelical community to recruit personnel who have certain desirable skills and abilities. This policy is ultimately detrimental to the integrity of Christian witness because it leads to confusion and compromise. How does your understanding of Ezra 4:1–3 help shape your understanding of what it means to discern dangers in proposals for partnership?

Overcoming opposition

Bible reading: Ezra 4

Focus on...

'When the enemies of Judah and Benjamin heard that the exiles were building a temple for the LORD, the God of Israel, they came to Zerubbabel and to the heads of the families and said, "Let us help you build because, like you, we seek your God and have been sacrificing to him since the time of Esarhaddon king of Assyria, who brought us here." But Zerubbabel, Jeshua and the rest of the heads of the families of Israel answered, "You have no part with us in building a temple to our God. We alone will build it for the LORD, the God of Israel, as King Cyrus, the king of Persia, commanded us." Then the peoples around them set out to discourage the people of Judah and make them afraid to go on building. They hired counsellors to work against them and frustrate their plans during the entire reign of Cyrus king of Persia and down to the reign of Darius king of Persia. At the beginning of the reign of Xerxes, they lodged an accusation against the people of Judah and Jerusalem.' (Ezra 4:1–6)

'Thus the work on the house of God in Jerusalem came to a standstill until the second year of the reign of Darius king of Persia.' (Ezra 4:24)

'Then, because of the decree King Darius had sent, Tattenai, governor of Trans-Euphrates, and Shethar-Bozenai and their associates carried it out with diligence. So the elders of the Jews continued to build and prosper under the preaching of Haggai the prophet and Zechariah, a descendant of Iddo. They finished building the temple according to the command of the God of Israel and the decrees of Cyrus, Darius and Artaxerxes, kings of Persia. The temple was completed on the third day of the month Adar, in the sixth year of the reign of King Darius.' (Ezra 6:13–15)

These verses encapsulate something in the history of Israel that ought to encourage us to engage enthusiastically in building for the glory of the Lord. God does not dwell in buildings, rather he inhabits the lives of those who invite him to reside and reign in their hearts. Paul was greatly distressed to see the Athenian idolatry and in his preaching against it he declared, 'The God who made the world and everything in it is the Lord of heaven and earth and does not live in temples built by hands' (Acts 17:24). The believer is the temple in which the Holy Spirit dwells as the apostle Paul tells us that God has 'put his Spirit in our hearts' (2 Cor. 1:22).

Paul reminds the Corinthians of this fact, *'Don't you know that you yourselves are God's temple and that God's Spirit lives in you?'* (1 Cor. 3:16). A few chapters on in the same epistle he emphasises the same point, *'Do you not know that your body is a temple of the Holy Spirit, who is in you, whom you have received from God?'* (1 Cor. 6:19). Paul felt it necessary to state and restate this amazing truth to a people who were engaged in practices that were compromising the integrity of the church and bringing the gospel into disrepute.

Committed to that work of construction

We should be committed to seeing that work of construction making progress. It is a work that has commenced; it is a work that is continuing; it is a work that will ultimately be brought to completion in the fullness of time. Peter also describes the believer as part of that edifice which is under construction when he says, *'you also, like living stones, are being built into a spiritual house…'* (1 Pet. 2:5).

While on a holiday in Barcelona one summer I visited the Temple de la Sagrada Familia. I hasten to add that, in so doing, I was neither paying homage at a shrine nor acknowledging the veracity of the particular theological tradition to which it belongs. Visiting this cathedral is very much like visiting the Eiffel Tower in Paris or the Statue of Liberty in New York. That towering landmark of Barcelona is still a work in progress, although it was begun in 1882. Its architect was the famous Antoni Gaudi. As I approached the site by bus I could see the great spires and the cranes and scaffolding in place. To say it was an ambitious vision is to understate the daunting task of construction that labours on.

Inside, I sat on a bench and looked around at this astonishing architectural adventure and feat of engineering. An elderly couple (tourists) sat beside me and the gentleman whispered, too audibly, 'I know it is a wonderful building, but back home, this project properly managed and financed would have been completed long ago.' The lady said nothing and I hoped her silence indicated disagreement. Afterwards I told my wife what I had heard and we had to agree that he was probably right but somehow it would not be the same. The product (a cathedral) would be achieved but much of the process would have been bypassed. This incident made me think of the fact that God is building his church and that he has unlimited resources and infinite skill. He could have clicked his fingers and the work would have been done. After all, the universe came into being at his command.

The almighty architect

The most interesting thing about the Temple de la Sagrada Familia is its architect, his vision and his sacrifice to achieve that vision. Its history, obstacles to its construction and the overcoming of those obstacles are extraordinary. Of course the architecture is fascinating too! What the gentleman on the bench failed to understand was that the process itself was amazing. Isn't this true in the history of the church? The great architect commenced the work. He laid out his vision and laid down his life for the achievement of that vision. He has left us to complete the work in accordance with his design. We encounter opposition and learn to overcome. He has given us gifts and we engage them in this service as we labour and toil. Neither the architect nor the labourers have seen its completion but the work in progress tells a story and everything is invested with significance.

Gaudi was run over by a tram and died in 1926 at the age of seventy-four, and the work was suspended for many years. Unforeseen events may sometimes bring the work to a standstill as happened with the Jewish exilic returnees: *'Thus the work on the house of God in Jerusalem came to a standstill until the second year of the reign of Darius king of Persia'* (Ezra 4:24). For a brief period immediately following the death of Christ the disciples were scattered and all seemed lost, but then they became aware of the resurrection and the Holy Spirit descended on them at Pentecost. The work continued with great pace in the power of the Holy Spirit but it is ongoing. We all dream of seeing it completed but which one of us would rather have avoided giving our time and talent to its construction?

Gaudi was just a man, a remarkable man, an exceptionally gifted man, but a man nonetheless. His work is temporal, and however enduring it may appear we know that it is ultimately, in the light of eternity, ephemeral. Jesus said, '*Heaven and earth will pass away, but my words will never pass away*' (Matt. 24:35). The church is being built on earth but it is being built for eternity. It is a work that is opposed by the world, the flesh and the devil. In the face of such opposition and the fear that it may induce we need to focus on the face of the Saviour. The writer to the Hebrews exhorts the saints to '*consider him who endured such opposition from sinful men, so that you will not grow weary and lose heart*' (Heb. 12:3). The Master is our model. The clear implication of this verse is that we ought to emulate Jesus, by the grace of God. Meditating on the master makes us interested in imitating him.

Work in Progress

Opposition is something that discourages us and we grow tired. When we feel like this we begin to think that this struggle is too difficult, even futile, and we may wish to concede defeat. When we are labouring in our own strength we become weary and feel isolated, as if we are alone in this task, or at least greatly outnumbered. It is at times such as this that we need to remember that God is with us. That is after all the meaning of the word 'Emmanuel.' We can be confident that we will overcome because he is with us. We may well apply the words of the prophet Isaiah to the enemies of the church, '*Devise your strategy, but it will be thwarted; propose your plan, but it will not stand, for God is with us*' (Is. 8:10).

Just as God was with the Israelites when they emerged from slavery in Egypt so he will be with us. His promise to them, '*I will be an enemy to your enemies and will oppose those who oppose you*' (Ex. 23:22) is reaffirmed to us in the promise, '"*Never will I leave you; never will I forsake you.*' So we say with confidence, "*The Lord is my helper; I will not be afraid. What can man do to me?*"' (Heb. 13:5–6). We have the constant companionship of Christ, his presence, power and provision. It is God's battle and we are not fighting *for* the victory, rather we are fighting *in* the victory. God declares his intention to set himself against those who resist us in our work for him. Those who argue and compete against his cause will ultimately have to face him.

Hannah's prayer strikes this note, *'He will guard the feet of his saints, but the wicked will be silenced in darkness. It is not by strength that one prevails; those who oppose the LORD will be shattered. He will thunder against them from heaven; the LORD will judge the ends of the earth'* (1 Sam. 2:9–10).

It is very easy to become discouraged when there is no evident progress in the project of the building of the kingdom. There are times when the work of the Lord in which we are engaged comes to a standstill, or at least it appears that way. These pauses may be perplexing. Unfinished work appears acceptable when it is progressing but when the work ceases it looks more like a problem than a project.

Planning permission

In a thinly populated rural area of West Cork in Ireland, a building project that had recently commenced had to cease before completion. The house was being constructed in a very scenic area overlooking one of West Cork's many sandy beaches. The site had been cleared, the foundations had been put in place and the walls of the dwelling had been about half finished. It remained in that condition for a long time because there had been an objection by local residents to the scale of the structure. Permission had been granted for building on the site but not to the dimensions to which the home was being constructed. As the owner/builder had not complied with the details of the permission granted by the planning authorities he had to remove some of the work done and begin again in accordance with the specified requirements. I'm sure it must have been an embarrassment. His plans were thwarted and I would imagine the additional cost of having to delay and demolish must have been a cause of some annoyance.

There was opposition to the work of God in Ezra's time, but we must remember that the people of Israel had received their planning permission not only from the highest secular authority but also from the highest authority of earth and heaven, namely from God. They were not breaching any regulations. They did not deviously deviate from the permission granted. This is also true of us who are engaged in fulfilling the great commission. Let us remind ourselves of these words of commissioning: *'Then Jesus came to them and said, "All authority in heaven and on earth has been given to me. Therefore go and make disciples of all nations, baptising them in the name of the Father and of the Son and of the Holy Spirit, and teaching them to obey everything I have commanded you. And surely I am with you always, to the very end of the age"'* (Matt. 28:18–20). Let us also remember that these words are from the highest authority and therefore no objections or opposition will ultimately be entertained.

In the face of opposition, in the home, at school, in the workplace or wherever it might be, we would do well to remember the promise of God to Joshua and its application to us today: *'Have I not commanded you? Be strong and courageous. Do not be terrified; do not be discouraged, for the LORD your God will be with you wherever you go'* (Josh. 1:9). It is required rather than requested of us that we have confidence in him and demonstrate that sense of security to others around us. In seeking to fulfil the obligations of this imperative we need to trust in the truth of the sufficiency of his grace. Sadly, fear is a familiar feeling and a very unpleasant emotion. The deep and natural desire to belong is threatened when we experience rejection and ridicule because of what we believe. But we must be prepared to stand up and be counted among those who are his disciples. The Holy Spirit dwells within us and he is the great comforter.

Questions: for discussion

1. Read Ezra 4:1–6,24 and Ezra 6:13–15. What encouragement might we derive from these verses?

2. Where does God dwell today? See Acts 17:24; 2 Cor. 1:22; 1 Cor. 3:16.

3. Consider the following verses: Is. 8:10; Heb. 13:5–6; 1 Sam. 2:9–10. In the face of opposition what comfort, strength and inspiration might we derive from such verses?

4. Who has commissioned us to make the gospel known? See Matt. 28:18–20 and discuss our commission in the light of Rom. 8:31.

5. Opposition to the work of the gospel can take many forms ranging from apathy to antipathy. It is easy to become discouraged. See Josh.

1:6–9 for words that stimulate courage and challenge complacency.

6. Our individual lives and the lives of our churches are a work in progress. What does it mean to be a stone in the hands of the master mason? See 1 Pet. 2:5 and think of the tools a mason uses to do his work.

Priests of psychology and prophets of pluralism

Bible reading: Ezra 4

Focus on...

'Then the peoples around them set out to discourage the people of Judah and make them afraid to go on building. They hired counsellors to work against them and frustrate their plans during the entire reign of Cyrus king of Persia and down to the reign of Darius king of Persia.' (Ezra 4:4–5)

In these verses we learn that God's enemies engage professional help by commissioning the services of 'counsellors'. It is likely that these counsellors were corrupt Persian officials who were offered some monetary or material inducement to thwart the plans of God's people. Here is a concerted campaign of harassment by a heathen community directed against the Hebrew cohort. The original language conveys the sense that this was a persistent problem. The result was very effective as we see in verse twenty-four of chapter four, 'Thus the work on the house of God in Jerusalem came to a standstill...' This determined effort to discourage was more than ridicule. Mocking and snide comments might well result in discouragement but these verses tell us that the kind of campaign waged against them made them 'afraid to go on building' (v. 4). This certainly suggests threats and intimidation. The people around them instilled fear in their hearts. The phrase 'make them afraid' in the Hebrew describes the kind of fear aroused in combat.

The *phrase 'set out to discourage'* may be translated as 'weakening the hands'. In other words they sought to disarm them by generating despondency. They were determined to undermine the work and they set about obstructing it by demoralising the workers. Their approach was to appeal to the authorities and make certain accusations. The nature of those accusations focuses on the potential political instability and economic repercussions of allowing the Israelites freedom to worship.

There are many places in the world today where such arguments are employed to suppress the people of God and deny them freedom of worship. Christianity is seen as a threat to the political stability of countries such as China, North Korea, and numerous Muslim countries in Asia and Africa such as Pakistan and The Sudan. In such countries spurious complaints are frequently processed through official channels.

We are in hostile territory

These people whom we read about in Ezra had a predisposed antipathy to the people of God. Their arguments were submitted to the appropriate authorities. Those who were outside the covenant relationship surrounded God's people. They were in hostile territory. The surrounding people were aware of the work that was taking place. It was not possible for them to be unaware of it. A building project of this nature was very conspicuous. There would have been a great deal of activity. In fact, the temple, although primarily a place of worship for God's people, was also a place of witness to the surrounding peoples.

We may be sure that the spiritual activity of believers today in building for God does not go unobserved in the community. There ought to be sufficient activity to be conspicuous. Our places of worship are also places of witness. Although in Western society there is political freedom to worship it is nonetheless true that many people find Christian work objectionable. In some of the worst case scenarios, outreach to children in the community has been described as 'proselytism'. Services have been described as 'fundamentalist Bible-bashing'. The Christian has been described as 'a narrow-minded bigot engaged in brainwashing'. The evangelical Christian is seen as 'right-wing and homophobic'. Many people find it incredible that evangelical Christians do not believe in the theory of evolution and as such the believer is seen as something akin to a person who believes the earth is flat and not spherical.

In a recent conversation in my home with the U.K. chief executive officer of the Christian apologetics ministry, Answers in Genesis, I learned of the active and very real opposition they face from influential intellectuals and religious leaders who are vehemently antagonistic to creation science. When we begin to construct a work for God we soon learn that it casts a shadow that people outside covenant relationship with God find objectionable. The Christian moral position on sexuality and sexual intimacy, for example, is thought to be rather backward because we do not believe in pre-marital, extra-marital or homosexual sex. Although evangelical Christianity is more acceptable in some cultures than others, nevertheless, when Christians uphold the biblical perspective on creation, sexuality, and the unique and universal claims of Christ there will be opposition. Jesus said, '*In this world you will have trouble. But take heart! I have overcome the world*' (John 16:33b).

God's people have enemies

God's people have enemies in today's world and these include the priests of psychology and the prophets of pluralism. Psychology has become the secular religious system of our age and tolerance is the dominant ethic of our times. There is no doubt that we have much to learn about the operations of the human mind, and professional psychology and psychiatry have a role to play in contributing to our understanding of mental welfare. However, we must be aware that many theoretical approaches to psychology are essentially atheistic and amoral.

The volume of sales for pop-psychology publications is an indication of the extent to which these people mediate their message that man is evolving, and part of that process will involve shedding the notion of God. Chat shows around the world host these priests who disseminate their secular message. Essentially they say that Christianity may have had its place in the past but now we have moved on from that and we know better. The Christian view is ridiculed and rejected. In our pluralistic society which embraces many minority groups and cultural traditions, psychological therapies are 'non-directive'. What evangelical Christians have to say on this issue is a challenge to the tolerance of a society that reveres tolerance as an essential virtue. The Christian voice may well sound strident in a society that insists on conformity to its norms. It is easy to be discouraged in such an environment. Like God's people in Ezra who set out with good intentions of being involved in this great building project, we too may find ourselves becoming despondent and our hands may be weakened to the point where we put down our tools and discontinue the work.

It is interesting to note that in our society certain words are seen as antiquated and undesirable. One such word is the word 'sin'. It is not politically correct to use the word 'sin'. It is not merely the word itself that is disallowed but the concept of sinfulness is rejected as a judgmental, medieval superstition. When the Christian uses biblical terms to describe certain attitudes and activities he is evoking the hostility of people in the surrounding community who do not share the same perspective. So, in society, euphemisms are coined and circulated to describe, for example, homosexuals as 'gay' and adultery as 'an affair'.

The Christian must speak the truth in love and demonstrate compassion to all sinners, for that is what we are, sinners saved by God's grace. We are the recipients of his unmerited favour and our ministry as believers is one of reconciliation. We are to do all that we can to see those who are estranged from God reconciled to him through Christ.

There are forces in society that seem to pull in opposite directions such as increasing secularisation and the rise of cults and fundamentalist religions. This is one of the conditions of postmodernism where apparent contradictions may be accommodated. This is evident in the fact that traditional Christian values are rejected as mere superstitions but new pagan practices are acceptable. Many people think that paganism is a pre-Christian stage of society but paganism exists in all ages. The term 'pagan' may refer to pantheists who believe that God is in all nature. Such people engage in worship that admits or tolerates all gods. Thus we have our modern-day pantheons. Pagans who are hostile to the truth that Jesus is the only way to heaven surround Christians today. They launch verbal missiles that often hit the target. Many people (of a certain generation) when they were children were taught by their parents to respond to taunting and name calling by their peers with these words 'sticks and stones will break my bones but names will never hurt me'. The truth is that names do hurt and sometimes have the effect of gagging or censoring believers. This is like the effect that the enemies of God's people had on the returnees who wanted to build but found their hands weakened by effective opposition.

Paganism is also a term used to describe the irreligious. Such a person is a heathen. If you are without *true* religion in one sense it is true that you have *no* religion at all. Thus our world is becoming increasingly pagan, where false religion, cults and new age philosophy abound. It is also a postmodern world where truth and morality are seen as relative rather than absolute and tolerance is the spirit of the age. We can be intimidated in such an environment and afraid to open our mouths to speak the truth. If it feels like the kind of fear induced by a battle situation that is because we are engaged in spiritual warfare. We can be ashamed of the gospel and gagged by fear of ridicule or rejection. It is easy to become disheartened in the face of such opposition.

Although the verses under consideration demonstrate that God's people were discouraged by a determined opposition from those outside the household of faith, it is a sad reality that sometimes discouragement comes from those within the covenant community. This displeases the Lord greatly. In the Old Testament we read of Moses being instructed by God to send some men to explore the Land of Canaan. A leader from each ancestral tribe was sent and ten out of the twelve men returned with a bad report. They focused on the problems rather than the potential. They felt powerless against the giants of the land and seemed to have forgotten the great power of their God.

Caleb and Joshua, on the other hand, realised that their God was great and that they could overcome in the strength he supplies, and they exhorted the people to enter the land and take possession of it. The lesson to be learned from this event is that some people see big problems and a little God whereas others see a big God and little problems. The believer should never find himself engaged in the service of the enemy who seeks to discourage God's people. We are exhorted in the New Testament to '*encourage one another daily*' (Heb. 3:13).

But the ten men spread their discouraging report, resulting in the people of God rebelling to such an extent that they expressed regret for leaving Egypt and talked about electing a leader to take them back to Egypt! Moses and Aaron tried to dissuade them from such a course of action and the people talked about stoning them! The people were very receptive to the negative report. The Lord's anger burned against them and the result was that the ten men were struck down with a fatal disease in a plague sent by the Lord. Not only that, but the entire population, with the exception of Joshua and Caleb, were deprived of the blessing that could have been theirs. They were condemned to wander in the wilderness for forty years. Their sin was 'unfaithfulness' (Num. 14:33). The Christian should be careful not to be seconded in the service of Satan. It is a terrible thing to discourage God's people.

The problem of pluralism

We live in a pluralist society that embraces many minority groups and cultural traditions. It is a very good thing to protect minorities, and all people must be allowed freedom of conscience and afforded opportunity to practise their religion without fear. We may disagree with the religious views of others but we must accept that in a healthy society there can be no place for racism, sectarianism or religious discrimination. However, it seems that we have surrendered to forces that will ultimately destabilise society by a process of moral fragmentation. Society feels obliged to accommodate every sort of perversion guided by the pagan priests of psychology.

So opposition today has its priests and prophets. They are the spokespeople and advocates of secularism and godless philosophy. They are the apologists of amorality. They are the idols of the music industry and the icons of fashion. They are the moguls of the media and the gurus of our generation. Psychology is the new religion and its godless counsel and man-centred pseudo-scientific therapies are inherently anti-religious. The enemies of God are diligently critiquing Christianity in every sphere of academia from the sciences to humanities. This postmodern matrix is promoting experimental alternatives especially in areas of education. Numerous theses are written in many universities in the name of scholarship and under the supervision of academics that present Christianity as nothing more than an oppressive and manipulative story that has failed humanity. We must not allow such opposition to discourage us and make us afraid to go on building.

The feminist perspective permeates academia too and pupils are perpetually processed through that paradigm. Let me tell you about a young man who submitted an assignment as part of his degree in English literature to his university lecturer (a feminist). The question posed was, 'Discuss Hamlet's relationship with Ophelia.' He was quite taken aback when his work was returned with the comment that he had neglected to deal with 'Hamlet's anti-feminine rhetoric toward Ophelia'. He knew then that no matter what the question the answer had to include a feminist perspective. Although feminism has many legitimate causes to advance in the area of women's rights and sexual equality it is also true that some influential feminist lobbies are seeking to promote their hidden agenda of lesbianism. Learning and scholarship are wonderful things but it is nevertheless true that academia unmasked leaves much to be desired.

There is a unity in the evil that seeks to subvert our plans to build for eternity and to the glory of God. But we take heart in the knowledge that God is the architect and builder of his church. He has said, *'I will build my church, and the gates of Hades will not overcome it'* (Matt. 16:18). We are not paranoid in thinking that the forces arrayed against us are determined to discredit God's people. We may be sure that our enemies are in league with the spiritual powers of darkness who seek to frustrate the work of God by discouraging the people of God who are engaged in this great building project. Let us remember, therefore, that *'our struggle is not against flesh and blood, but against the rulers, against the authorities, against the powers of this dark world and against the spiritual forces of evil in the heavenly realms'* (Eph. 6:12). But let us also bear in mind that we have been granted planning permission for this building project by the supreme emperor of the universe. Our authority comes from the mightiest monarch who is our beloved Master. It is on record that we have been commissioned to this work of construction (Matt. 28:18–20). So let us take heart and not be discouraged or afraid.

Questions: for discussion

1. What does it mean to be an alien in this world? See John 16:33b; Heb. 11:13; 1 Pet. 1:1,17; 1 Pet. 2:11. In what circumstances do you feel like an outsider?
2. Should the Christian speak out against society's slide into perversity? See Matt. 5:13–14 and discuss the implications for today.

3. What is the appropriate tone in addressing social issues from the Christian perspective? See Eph. 4:15 and discuss the necessity for both 'truth' and 'love' and how one may be distorted by overemphasising the other.

4. See Eph. 6:12. It is easy to become discouraged in the face of such organised, determined and powerful opposition. How does Matt. 16:18 give us an eternal perspective?

5. The pluralist agenda has been too successful in silencing the Christian voice on moral issues. There are infinite opportunities to speak out against this trend by intelligently discussing films, advertising and social issues from a Christian perspective. Discuss where these opportunities might arise and how you can best prepare to engage non-Christians in discussion. See 1 Pet. 3:15.

6. It seems that the moral decline of society is reflected in the language used to describe and define certain activity. What can the Christian do to ensure that he/she maintains a healthy spiritual perspective? See 1 Cor. 6:9–11.

Trouble, teaching and trowels

Bible reading: Ezra 5

Focus on...

'Now Haggai the prophet and Zechariah the prophet, a descendant of Iddo, prophesied to the Jews in Judah and Jerusalem in the name of the God of Israel, who was over them. Then Zerubbabel son of Shealtiel and Jeshua son of Jozadak set to work to rebuild the house of God in Jerusalem. And the prophets of God were with them, helping them.' (Ezra 5:1–2)

The fourth chapter ends on a rather discouraging note. In verse twenty-four of that chapter we read these words: 'the work on the house of God in Jerusalem came to a standstill.' Their great vision had now become obscured. Their minds must have been shrouded in disappointment and doubt. Their hopes and all that they had been working toward came to an end, or so it seemed for a while. But God spoke into this bleak situation and it was transformed. At the sound of his voice the universe came into being and now that same God spoke to them through the prophets Haggai and Zechariah. It is truly amazing how the Word of God can transform people. This discouraged and fearful people were changed into warriors who wielded trowels in the battle to build for the glory of God! They were a troubled people who overcame their difficulties by adhering to the teaching of God's spokesmen and engaging in practical work toward the achievement of their goal to establish temple worship in the midst of hostile onlookers and active opponents.

Learning the lessons

There is a lesson to be learned in this for every child of God. One such lesson is that in times of trouble when the work of God is opposed and the believer's heart is fearful he may take encouragement from the Word of God and continue to labour in love for the glory of the Almighty. How many times in your experience has the Word of God dispelled doubt and discouragement? How often has the Word of God broken the spell of backsliding and addressed the apostasy of your heart? When was the last time you allowed the Word of God to free you from fear? The Word can appease our anxieties and calm our concerned hearts. It is a Word that can inspire indifferent hearts and nourish the needy heart. The Word raises our eyes to righteousness and tames the tempest that torments the soul.

Obeying God rather than men

There was an important issue to be addressed here for the people of God. God had commissioned them to do a work and that work had begun well, but it was brought to a standstill by the opposition of a secular authority. Whom should they obey? If God authorises a work and the secular powers oppose that work what are the people of God to do? Are there any circumstances in which the people of God should disobey the authorities, or is that a subversive approach which is prohibited in Scripture? Let us examine the Word of God to obtain some clarity on this issue.

The people of Israel had been oppressed in captivity in Egypt at a much earlier point in their history. They had cruel slave masters who forced them to build for Pharaoh. They were treated ruthlessly but ultimately they were redeemed from that evil empire. However, at one point the king of Egypt instructed the midwives Shiphrah and Puah: *'When you help the Hebrew women in childbirth and observe them on the delivery stool, if it is a boy, kill him; but if it is a girl, let her live'* (Ex. 1:16). Here you have a secular power giving an immoral instruction to commit infanticide and it is clearly evil. It is instructive to note how these women responded to such a command: *'The midwives, however, feared God and did not do what the king of Egypt had told them to do; they let the boys live'* (v. 17). It is clear from this that God approved of their refusal to obey the king. So we read in verses 20–21, *'So God was kind to the midwives and the people increased and became even more numerous. And because the midwives feared God, he gave them families of their own.'* Clearly then the people of God must never commit evil ordered by or accommodated by any authority.

There is further evidence in the New Testament of the limitations of secular authority. In Acts chapter four we read about Peter and John being seized and imprisoned for preaching the gospel. The next day the rulers, elders and the teachers of the law (including the high priest) interrogated them. In the eighteenth verse we read that they *'commanded them not to speak or teach at all in the name of Jesus.'* But listen to the fearless reply of Peter and John, *'Judge for yourselves whether it is right in God's sight to obey you rather than God. For we cannot help speaking about what we have seen and heard'* (vv. 19–20). This rhetorical question addresses the very issue we are considering—whether it is right to obey the authorities if they command us to ignore our commission from God. The clear implication of these Scriptures is that it would be entirely inappropriate to capitulate to such pressure.

If we are in any doubt about this matter the next chapter in Acts makes it crystal clear. Here the apostles are being questioned before the high priest and the full assembly of the elders of Israel. The apostles were reminded that they had been given strict instructions not to preach in the name of Jesus and that they now stood accused of flagrantly violating the clear command of the authorities. But they did not cower in submission. Rather, we read, *'Peter and the other apostles replied: "We must obey God rather than men!"'* (v. 29). This should always to be our guiding principle.

Respecting the law

However, the people of God are subject to the law in every other area apart from anything that would be a violation of God's law or inhibit the dissemination of the gospel. This is clearly the teaching of Scripture: *'Everyone must submit himself to the governing authorities…'* (Rom. 13:1). We are not to be rebellious against the law and we should bear in mind that *'…he who rebels against the authority is rebelling against what God has instituted…'* (Rom. 13:2). In his letter to Titus Paul emphasised the necessity for instruction in civil obedience: *'Remind the people to be subject to rulers and authorities'* (Titus 3:1). In fact the people of God are exhorted to engage in intercessory prayer for the civic powers of this world. Paul implored Timothy to pray for the authorities: *'I urge, then, first of all, that requests, prayers, intercession and thanksgiving be made for everyone—for kings and all those in authority, that we may live peaceful and quiet lives in all godliness and holiness. This is good, and pleases God our Saviour, who wants all men to be saved and to come to a knowledge of the truth'* (1 Tim. 2:1–4).

We ought not to forget the earthly dimension to the authority of Christ for he himself said, *'All authority in heaven and on earth has been given to me…'* (Matt. 28:18). It is our spiritual and civil duty to obey those in authority except where that government or law contradicts the law of God and/or seeks to gag the people of God by forbidding them from spreading the gospel. Therefore we must recognise that there may be exceptional and limited circumstances in which it is appropriate to disobey the law.

Many of God's people in today's world find themselves in the reality of such circumstances. In a recent preaching visit to Moldova I met people who had suffered under the communist system. They had learned to circumvent the discriminatory and anti-Christian laws of their land. They had clandestine services in spite of communist inspired laws prohibiting such meetings. Such situations are well documented and the Western church has traditionally supported their activity through various missionary agencies. The church still supports Christians in places where it is illegal to meet in the name of Jesus or distribute the Scriptures. There are many such countries. In the Muslim world Christians are engaged in surreptitious missionary activity for fear of deportation, imprisonment, torture or death. The anti-Christian laws of Islamic states are themselves unjust and cannot be observed by God's people who feel impelled to speak of the glorious gospel of God.

Dealing with discouragement

So the prophets Haggai and Zechariah exhorted the Israelites to obey God and not to yield to the pressure to cease the work altogether. Encouraged by their prophetic ministry, the people of God who had temporarily discontinued their labours recommenced their activity in the name of their God. Pagan authorities had given the approval to build but then withdrew that consent. In such circumstances it is necessary to behave wisely, as in fact they do. However, the cessation of the work should be seen, primarily, as a moment of weakness in the lives of the otherwise commendable men who had commenced it. Although God's people are to try to work within the law, in the context it is clear that they ought not to have stopped the work on the edict of the reigning king because he did not have supreme authority in this matter. The divine decree could not be disregarded by the word of any earthly ruler.

The words of the prophets held before them the supreme authority of the Word of God in regulating their affairs. The prophets reminded them of the divine government and the supreme sovereign. Their relationship as subjects to that supremacy of rule could not be overlooked. It was a difficult situation but when it is viewed in the light of the divine will and wisdom it is seen in proper perspective. Perspective is about having the right impression of relative positions. The people of God momentarily lost sight of this spiritual view of the relative importance of things. Their sense of proportion was distorted and they forgot who God was. They had the authority of the emperor of the universe yet feared the relatively petty power of this underling! His power was real enough to induce compliance with his order and no doubt the penalty for non-compliance would have been grave. But true spiritual perspective must keep the wishes of even the kings of this world subordinate to the authority of the Almighty.

Inspired by the prophetic teaching of Haggai and Zechariah, they began the work again and carried it through to completion. Opposition continued but through the influence of the Word of God their consciousness was altered. Their understanding of their covenant relationship to God was restored and they went forward despite the presence of powerful foes.

God's people need this sense of proportion in every generation. That sense of who God is and a right relationship to him is vital in pressing forward in the presence of powerful foes. It is the Word of God that brings that perspective into focus. May his Word prevail in our hearts dispelling fear and inspiring greater endeavour in the work of the kingdom! In times of trouble may we adhere to the teaching of the Word and wield the trowel in building for eternity.

Questions: for discussion
1. Why did the presence of the prophets encourage the people?

2. What is the appropriate Christian attitude to the law? See Rom. 13:1–2; Tit. 3:1; 1 Tim. 2:1–4.
3. Are there any exceptional circumstances in which it might be appropriate to ignore the law? See Ex. 1:1–21; Acts 4:19–20; Acts 5:29.
4. How can the Christian encourage clandestine ministry in Muslim countries?
5. It was the Word of God that influenced the attitudes of God's people in Ezra's day. Are we prepared to allow the Word of God to alter our consciousness and strengthen our resolve? What opportunities do we have to allow Scripture to mould us?
6. What is the role and function of the believer in society? Discuss the nature and scope of that role in the light of the great commission (Matt. 28:18–20).

The secret of success

Bible reading: Ezra 6

Focus on...

'So the elders of the Jews continued to build and prosper under the preaching of Haggai the prophet and Zechariah, a descendant of Iddo. They finished building the temple according to the command of the God of Israel and the decrees of Cyrus, Darius and Artaxerxes, kings of Persia. The temple was completed on the third day of the month Adar, in the sixth year of the reign of King Darius. Then the people of Israel—the priests, the Levites and the rest of the exiles—celebrated the dedication of the house of God with joy.' (Ezra 6:14–16)

Worship and witness

T he temple was a place for worship and witness. It is the privilege of those who have been freed from captivity to ensure that the name of God is exalted among those outside the household of faith. So every believer must take seriously his responsibility to engage in building a testimony to the glory of God. The secret of their success is not in fact a secret at all: 'So the elders of the Jews continued to build and prosper under the preaching of Haggai the prophet and Zechariah...' (v. 14). Rather, it is the key to their success as it will be the key to ours. The people of God always prosper when they adhere to the Word of God. How often in Scripture we see the other side of this coin when God's people refuse to listen to the prophets and rebel against his righteous counsel. In such situations, which are all too numerous in Scripture, the consequences are catastrophic. What a joy it is, therefore, to read of the people of God thriving by trusting in the eternal wisdom and efficacy of his revealed will. What was it that they preached? Whatever the message was, it made a difference. So let us take a closer look at the content of that authoritative and anointed proclamation.

Dealing with disinterest

Haggai and Zechariah were contemporaries in the post-exilic period of the sixth century BC. Let us consider the preaching of Haggai. In this period of post-captivity he rebuked the returned exiles for their delay in rebuilding the Temple and he also encouraged them to engage in the work of rebuilding. The work of construction that had begun well was discontinued not only because of opposition from hostile observers, but also because of disinterest on the part of the people of God. The people had begun to build houses for themselves and so the work of rebuilding the Temple was neglected. Thus we read in Haggai, *'Then the word of the LORD came through the prophet Haggai: "Is it a time for you yourselves to be living in your panelled houses, while this house remains a ruin?"'* (Hag. 1:3–4).

Haggai stepped into this scene of misguided priorities to exhort the people to put first things first. *'Now this is what the LORD Almighty says: "Give careful thought to your ways"'* (Hag. 1:5). He urged them to make the rebuilding of the Temple a priority. *'"Go up into the mountains and bring down timber and build the house, so that I may take pleasure in it and be honoured," says the LORD'* (Hag. 1:8). His message was that God's work must not be neglected, so he counselled them to consider their ways and finish what they had started. It is a message with contemporary relevance because it calls on us to take stock of our own commitment by considering what we have done in the Lord's work thus far, what we have neglected to do and what we ought to do.

Blessing had been withheld because the people had failed to put God first. *'"You expected much, but see, it turned out to be little. What you brought home, I blew away. Why?" declares the LORD Almighty. "Because of my house, which remains a ruin, while each of you is busy with his own house. Therefore, because of you the heavens have withheld their dew and the earth its crops. I called for a drought on the fields and the mountains, on the grain, the new wine, the oil and whatever the ground produces, on men and cattle, and on the labour of your hands"'* (Hag. 1:9–11). Through the prophetic preaching of Haggai and Zechariah God stirred up enthusiasm for the project. They heard and heeded the Word of God and came together as a community of committed people. Prophets, priests and people worked together as a team in advancing God's aims.

The challenge to faith is the same in every generation. *'But seek first his kingdom and his righteousness, and all these things will be given to you as well'* (Matt. 6:33). We must consider the cost of discipleship and not allow the righteous work of God to be discontinued because of ridicule by onlookers. Jesus told those who flocked to him to consider their commitment. *'Suppose one of you wants to build a tower. Will he not first sit down and estimate the cost to see if he has enough money to complete it? For if he lays the foundation and is not able to finish it, everyone who sees it will ridicule him, saying, "This fellow began to build and was not able to finish"'* (Luke 14:28–30).

We have looked at the kind of opposition that came from outsiders and the discouragement it produced but within their own ranks there was disinterest. One of the greatest forms of opposition to the work of God today is the disinterest of God's people. How many are prepared to suspend their involvement in church activity while they build their careers? Everybody was wrapped up in his own selfish concerns and God was neglected. It is interesting to note that we are often distracted from the affairs of the kingdom by legitimate concerns rather than the lure of carnality. In other words good things can keep us from playing our part and fulfilling our duty to the Almighty. Genuine interests become gross indulgences when they displace God from that central role in our lives.

The glory of God

The real glory of the Temple was not in the cost of its precious metals and fine craftsmanship. Those things represented a God of beauty, order, purity and so on. The glory of the Temple was the presence of God in it. The glory of any project we pursue will only come from the presence of God in that work. *'Unless the LORD builds the house, its builders labour in vain'* (Ps. 127:1). The clear keynote of Haggai's preaching is that the redeemed remnant must reorder its priorities and engage in the work of building for God. This message applies to the believer today. Putting the work of the kingdom first is a necessary prerequisite to experiencing the blessing of God in our lives as individuals and as a church.

The foundations had been put in place but time had elapsed and the work had ceased. In the previous chapter we read, *'And the prophets of*

God were with them, helping them' (*Ezra* 5:2). The prophets were God's representatives and the people had the presence of these men to encourage them. Thus Haggai and Zechariah brought the assurance of God's presence to this discouraged and distracted people. *'Then Haggai, the LORD's messenger, gave this message of the LORD to the people: "I am with you," declares the LORD'* (Hag. 1:13). However, in the passage we are focusing on we read, *'So the elders of the Jews continued to build and prosper under the preaching of Haggai the prophet and Zechariah...'* It is clear that it is not just the presence of these men that led to the resumption of work but it was the preaching of the prophets and their message that spurred the people on. The message then was the same as it is now; half-hearted obedience will never result in God's wholehearted blessing.

God's grand scheme

These people were significant in God's grand scheme of things. Consider Zerubbabel, he is listed in the genealogical records of both Matthew and Luke. We too are significant in God's plans, more significant, perhaps than we would dare to imagine. If only we could catch a glimpse of the importance of the work of the kingdom and realise something of its eternal significance. It is wonderful to witness the positive effect of the preaching of the prophets in the lives of the people. They were stirred up to resume the work, confident in the knowledge that God is with them. What will be our response to the call to reorder our priorities? God promised future glory: *'"I will shake all nations, and the desired of all nations will come, and I will fill this house with glory...The glory of this present house will be greater than the glory of the former house," says the LORD Almighty'* (Hag. 2:7). And he has promised us no less: *'Now there is in store for me the crown of righteousness, which the Lord, the righteous Judge, will award to me on that day—and not only to me, but also to all who have longed for his appearing'* (2 Tim. 4:8). Those who are pleased to work for the glory of God will be rewarded.

Dealing with dissatisfaction

We have seen how God's people may be discouraged and disinterested but they may also be dissatisfied. The older ones who remembered the former glory of Solomon's Temple evaluated the new endeavour in the light of that magnificent structure, and the contrasts were more striking than the comparisons. Haggai asks them, *'Does it not seem to you like nothing?'* (Hag. 2:3). It is possible to have a glorious ideal by which we critically evaluate the activity of others. We may be dissatisfied with anything that falls short of that standard. However insignificant a work may appear we may be certain that the Lord can bless it and make it a glorious thing. We should not, therefore, despise small things. If God is in it then that work is great and glorious.

Explaining God's Word

In chapter seven of Ezra we read of Ezra's arrival in Jerusalem with the second contingent of returnees who would be involved in the work of restoration. In chapters eight to ten of Nehemiah we read of the great revival that took place under Ezra, the man whose name is given to the book we are exploring. We will take a closer look at this fascinating man in later chapters. For the moment it is important to focus on the role he played in determining the success of the repatriation project. In the eighth chapter of Nehemiah we learn that Ezra read and explained the law. The people listened attentively for several hours while *'Ezra the scribe stood on a high wooden platform built for the occasion...Ezra opened the book. All the people could see him because he was standing above them; and as he opened it, the people all stood up. Ezra praised the LORD, the great God; and all the people lifted their hands and responded, "Amen! Amen!" Then they bowed down and worshiped the LORD with their faces to the ground'* (vv. 4–6). The AV says, *'And Ezra the scribe stood upon a pulpit of wood, which they had made for the purpose...'* (v. 4). They built a pulpit because they wanted to hear what God had to say to them. What a great joy and privilege it is to step into a pulpit made by a people conscious of their need for the Word of God. What a thrill it is to look out on the faces of God's people and see a genuine hunger for his Word. They gave the Word, its public reading and explanation (preaching) an elevated position because they had a heart to have that Word rule over them. We read in those chapters how the people were instructed and obeyed and this is always the key to success in the spiritual life and it is also the secret of true happiness. Thus we read, *'And their joy was very great'* (Neh. 8:17).

Prophesy and preaching

It is not right to make a direct connection between the prophet and the preacher: *'In the past God spoke to our forefathers through the prophets at many times and in various ways, but in these last days he has spoken to us by his Son...'* (Heb. 1:1–2). However, there is a sense in which preaching is prophetic. When the preaching of the Word of God is a faithful exposition of the text of God's Word, it is a forth-telling of the mind of God as revealed in that Word, and that is often what the prophets were engaged in doing. This is not the same as a foretelling of future events, which was a unique prophetic function under the direction of God. But even in this regard the preacher may say with certainty, for example, that the unrepentant sinner is condemned to spend eternity in hell or that the Lord will return. The Lord has revealed to us, through his Word, something of the future. In this the preacher is not predicting the future, rather, he is proclaiming it. There are parallels in the roles of prophet and preacher but that is not to say they are the same. In the preacher's experience there are times when messages have prepared the hearts of God's people for events that were about to take place in their lives. It is not that the preacher has some kind of foreknowledge that those events would take place, but God condescended to minister to others in this way through the preaching of his own precious word.

The preacher, however, has feet of clay and so all that he says must be examined in the light of Scripture. The only difference between a soapbox and a pulpit is the Word of God. If the preacher is merely airing his views and flogging his hobbyhorses then he is not preaching at all! Preaching involves an exposition of the biblical text within wider and widest contexts.

The very architecture of most evangelical churches articulates our view of preaching. The pulpit is central and elevated because authoritative preaching is central to our practice and held in high regard. Thus the furniture speaks eloquently of our theology. However, I wonder if we are silently witnessing the passing of something sacred? Preaching is being devalued and sidelined. Therapeutic rather than theological messages are sought and self-esteem has been cultivated instead of self-examination in the light of Scripture. There is a shift from theological and expository preaching (which is seen as a tedious, moralising discourse) to therapeutic and empathetic epilogues.

'*So the elders of the Jews continued to build and prosper under the preaching of Haggai the prophet and Zechariah...*' (v. 14). Zechariah preached solemn warnings to the people and called them to repentance. He exhorted them not to repeat the mistakes of the past and we too ought to pay heed to such instruction.

Questions: for discussion

1. What role did the Word of God play in shaping the attitude and actions of the people of God? See Ezra 6:14–16.

2. What is the primary role of the church? See John 4:23 and Acts 1:8. Discuss this question in relation to worship and evangelism.

3. How would you define 'success' in the Christian life? What is the key to this 'success' and what are the obstacles to achieving it?

4. Compare and contrast the respective roles of both prophet and preacher. See pp.113–114 only after some discussion on the issue.

5. See 1 Tim. 6:6 and discuss the attitude of dissatisfaction in the light of this verse.

6. Zechariah exhorted the people not to repeat the mistakes of the past and we too ought to pay heed to such instruction. See 1 Cor. 10:9–11. What were the consequences of the grumbling discontent of the Israelites? What does Paul want us to learn from their mistakes?

Preaching for progress

Bible reading: Nehemiah 8

Focus on...

'All the people assembled as one man in the square before the Water Gate. They told Ezra the scribe to bring out the Book of the Law of Moses, which the LORD had commanded for Israel. So...Ezra the priest brought the Law before the assembly, which was made up of men and women and all who were able to understand. He read it aloud from daybreak till noon...And all the people listened attentively...Ezra the scribe stood on a high wooden platform built for the occasion...Ezra opened the book. All the people could see him because he was standing above them; and as he opened it, the people all stood up. Ezra praised the LORD, the great God; and all the people lifted their hands and responded, "Amen! Amen!" Then they bowed down and worshiped the LORD with their faces to the ground. The Levites...instructed the people in the Law while the people were standing there. They read from the Book of the Law of God, making it clear and giving the meaning so that the people could understand what was being read...all the people had been weeping as they listened to the words of the Law...The Levites calmed all the people, saying...Do not grieve. Then all the people went away...to celebrate with great joy, because they now understood the words that had been made known to them.' (Nehehiam 8:1–12)

H ere we go outside the book of Ezra to the eighth chapter of Nehemiah where we read of the great revival that took place under Ezra. What an astonishing record it is! It is very profitable to read the entire chapter to see the place of preaching in that situation. Before the Word of God was read Ezra led the people in praising God. These verses tell us that he 'praised the LORD, the great God.' He had a true sense of the majesty of God and this coloured his view of everything else. In a later chapter we shall see how, when he grieved because of the sin of the people, they saw the heart of God reflected in his grief and turned from their wickedness. Here in this passage we see a man who not only had a sense of the majesty of God, but who also instilled that sense of who God is within the hearts of the people. Before Scripture is read and explained it is essential that the man in the pulpit has a true awareness of the greatness of God. Theological acumen without this consciousness is inadequate. What happened when Ezra praised God? Verse six tells us that 'all the people lifted their hands and responded, "Amen! Amen!" Then they bowed down and worshiped the LORD with their faces to the ground.' There was a genuine response from the people. In order to give public expression to their unity of mind that God is indeed worthy to be praised as the great God of heaven and earth they lifted their hands and cried out "Amen! Amen!" These were a people who had not had opportunity for public worship in Babylon and they are overwhelmed by the occasion. They prostrate themselves on the ground and their physical posture reflects their attitude of heart. They are submissive, receptive and responsive. They are certainly focused on God and not themselves. It is only when we catch a glimpse of his awesome majesty that our hearts are filled with an abject awareness of our own inadequacies and unworthiness. Putting their faces in the dirt and assuming a lowly posture eloquently mimes their humility in his presence.

Reverence for the Word of God

They desire to hear the Word of God read aloud and explained and they listen intently to understand its meaning. It is as if they have come to hear the last will and testament of a close relative or friend being read aloud.

Again we see that there is great unity of purpose as the *people 'assembled as one man.'* It was the people who instructed Ezra to *'bring out the Book of the Law'* (v. 1). They were conscious of their unique history and how God had communicated with Moses, and they desired to be part of that continuity. They were very aware that this book had a moral imperative in its message to them. They wanted to know what it said and what they should do in order to observe its obligations. It was for them the *'Book of the Law of Moses, which the LORD had commanded for Israel.'* As such it was central to their identity. It explained their origin, their history, their nature, their destiny and the uniqueness of their relationship with God. They wanted to be guided and governed by its content.

So here we have this great assembly of people (men and women) and when the book was opened they stood up. Once again their physical posture reveals a certain attitude of heart. They were attentive and standing reflects this. Sitting is a more casual and relaxed posture but standing shows a certain reverence. Imagine that you are in a room when royalty or some civic dignitary entered that room. What would be your immediate response? Surely it would be to stand and by so doing to acknowledge your respect for the office/person. When the national anthem is sung we rise to our feet in acknowledgement of its significance. It is part of our unique identity and we acknowledge together its binding and unifying theme. So it was with these people, the Word was their anthem!

Ezra *'read it aloud from daybreak till noon'* (v. 3). The reading and exposition of the Word of God was central to the occasion. It dominated their time and their thinking. It was by any reckoning a very lengthy undertaking. This tells us a great deal about the seriousness of the people and the leadership regarding the Word of God. There is nothing casual about their attitude to it. It is wonderful to encounter people who have a genuine hunger for the Word of God. I have had the privilege of preaching in various churches in different cultures and I am astonished and humbled by the attitude of some people to the Word of God. In many Eastern European countries the preaching goes on for hours and the services are all-day affairs. I have preached in Eastern Europe where it is common for several sermons to be delivered in one service. Here we read that *'all the people listened attentively.'* It does not say that *some* of them listened attentively but that *all* of them listened attentively.

The view from pulpit and pew

As a preacher looks out on the congregation he sees different facial expressions. Some are attentive, some are distracted and some are tired. It is a great encouragement to the preacher to see everybody attentive to the Word of God. I wonder if sometimes people think of the sermon as something that has to be endured. Do some people feel relieved when the sermon comes to an end? It is a great thing to hear the Word of God expounded by a gifted preacher. The reading of Scripture comes alive as it is read with insight and passion. You can tell that such a man is familiar with this passage and could probably recite it without looking at the page. You feel that it is humility on his part to maintain eye contact with the text. When he looks into your face he seems to penetrate into your soul. And as he begins to explain the meaning of the passage it all makes perfect sense. It is not a lecture or a dissertation on a theme. There is something in his voice, something indescribable that rings true. He knows what he is talking about. It is authentic and authoritative. He is like the captain at the helm of the ship in a storm, focused and unafraid and as you look into his face you know that all is well. Such a preacher has a serenity and certainty in his voice. When we listen to preaching like that we know God's servant will bring the ship to port as he has done many times before. I like to think of Ezra like that as he stepped into the pulpit. The people recognised that he knew what they needed to know and they were going to give him every opportunity to tell them, tell it all and tell it again!

A word from above

We have already (in the previous chapter) drawn attention to the fact that the 'high wooden platform built for the occasion' or the 'pulpit of wood, which they had made for the purpose' had both pragmatic and symbolic significance. It is crucially important in the context of the contemporary church that we develop this theme further. We have seen that at the pragmatic level it was important that Ezra should be clearly visible to all those assembled to hear the public reading and exposition of the Word of God. However, the people were well aware that it was God's Word and not the words of Ezra or Moses. So, we re-emphasise the point that at the symbolic level they see this Word as something above them because they acknowledge its authority over them and they readily accept help in understanding it. We have already seen that it was with such an attitude that they came to listen. Thus we have come to understand that the elevated platform was a pragmatic structure that enabled the people to behold the preacher. But more than that, it had a symbolic significance in that it represented their understanding of their subordinate relationship to the superior Word of God. Refreshed on this point we now proceed to examine the issue in relation to the church today.

Preaching is a vital activity in the life of a healthy church. Wherever there is the faithful exposition of the Word of God there is spiritual strength. Wherever it is absent there is weakness. Evangelical churches that move away from the practice of regular preaching are becoming theologically foggy, non-doctrinal and all-inclusive. In such churches there is an appeal to feelings that puts emotions at the centre of their practice. Sadly we are beginning to see a consumerist attitude where the church has become a spiritual supermarket and there is a shift of emphasis from truth to technique. In this market-driven and consumer-oriented culture psychology tends to eclipse Christology and the transcendent truth of the gospel is trivialised. In the absence of authoritative proclamation other things have filled the vacuum.

We cannot dismiss the Word of God as irrelevant in society because God says that his Word will never be void of power: 'As *the rain and the snow come down from heaven, and do not return to it without watering the earth and making it bud and flourish, so that it yields seed for the sower and bread for the eater, so is my word that goes out from my mouth: It will not return to me empty, but will accomplish what I desire and achieve the purpose for which I sent it*' (Is. 55:10–11). There is tremendous encouragement in these words for any man committed to biblically informed, Christ-centred and Holy Spirit anointed preaching.

Market-driven messages

It is perfectly reasonable to examine different ways of communicating with our contemporaries. However, we must be careful not to yield to the temptation to market ourselves to 'unchurched' consumers by appealing to their emotions and forsaking the duty to teach people to think biblically. One of the aims of preaching is to enable people to model the message so that God's glory might be mirrored in a world that is stumbling about in darkness.

People seem to want sound-bites rather than sermons. But the church needs preachers of sound doctrine. It is interesting to note that Scripture identifies all sorts of ungodliness and irreligious attitudes such as adultery, perversion, slave trading, lying and perjury as '*contrary to the sound doctrine*' (1 Tim. 1:10).

Expository preaching is a form of spiritual discourse that dictates and regulates the content of the communication. Advocates of other forms of ecclesiology that minimise and displace preaching fail to recognise the inadequacy of alternative methodologies to shape and safeguard the message. At first we are urged to make what may appear to be cosmetic changes, and we soon discover that the content of our message is subordinate to its style of presentation. This is part of a dumbing-down process where the supporters, adherents, and defenders of the anti-preaching lobby are in effect promoting the use of optional means of transmitting the message. Means such as stringing comments and choruses together in a kind of spiritual necklace to adorn a church that is prostituting itself to the world instead of preaching to it! Paul's instruction to the Roman church needs to be restated in today's hedonistic society: '*Do not conform any longer to the pattern of this world, but be transformed by the renewing of your mind…*' (Rom. 12:2).

Preaching produces serious-minded and biblically informed people whereas in its absence there is shallowness. We must not refashion our ecclesiology to make ourselves more attractive and acceptable. Preaching is seen, in some circles, as no more than a cultural bias. But when we consider the fact that we live in an age of relativism, preaching as a means of prophetic proclamation has a healthy influence on churches where it is central to its life.

Authoritative preaching makes demands on its hearers and one is never left merely impressed with the eloquence of the preacher. A sermon is more than semantics. The hearer is made aware of the clear implications of the message. It is not the sensuous experience of the preaching or the superior logic of the argument but the power of the Holy Spirit that is at work. It is a cognitive communication and an emotional experience, but primarily it is a spiritual awakening and quickening of the soul. In other words, preaching is not just rhetoric; it has a spiritual resonance that vibrates in the soul. As believers, it trains us to tutor our minds and integrate our experience in a process that shapes our identity by defining and regulating our understanding of the truth in accordance with biblical patterns. But it requires in the hearer a residual faith in the authenticity and authority of the message as well as the medium of communication.

The church is like a river

Many cities are built beside rivers that form dominant features of the geographical landscapes where they are situated. Rivers traditionally have been part of the recreational and occupational life of people. But in one lifetime many great waterways have been slowly polluted and are no longer suitable for bathing. It is amazing what can be lost in a generation.

The church is like a river insofar as changes in its life are sometimes gradual and imperceptible at first. Like the river it can be slowly polluted. It takes time before the river becomes so poisonous that the fish die. Yet the river looks the same as before and one could still take a boat ride on it. In other words, even when life has been taken from it the river does not disappear, nor do all of its uses but its value has been diminished and its degraded condition will have harmful effects throughout the landscape.

Boating is now a leisure activity on many rivers, but in a previous generation the fish caught in those waterways sustained life. The rivers are still there but they are not what they used to be, they are not what they appear to be, and they are not what they should be! So it is with the church that is being slowly polluted. If a church merely has a recreational function in the life of the community it has ceased to be what it ought to be. In some churches an ephemeral and experiential enterprise masquerading as preaching has replaced the traditional sermon. The transcendent has been displaced by the trivial.

Preaching helps us ask the right questions

Preaching is not meant to be inert. It is not merely about imparting information. There has to be an information-action ratio where relevant information is generated into action, otherwise the information is no more than an abundance of irrelevant facts. Although in any communication environment input will always exceed output. In other words, what one is informed about will always exceed the possibility of action based on that information. The question is: what exactly should that ratio be? What is our expectation?

Detractors of preaching will say that we are faced with the problem of an information glut, which is another way of saying that there is diminished spiritual potency. They might suggest that the Sunday evening sermons dislodge the Sunday morning sermons from our minds. Surely, if this is true it is not less information that we need but more action.

People who say we are receiving answers to questions we did not ask are forgetting that preaching will help us to ask the right questions and not merely provide us with the answers to the questions we are asking!

The desire to be inoffensive

It no longer seems strange now for some to have church events where there is no preaching. Take, for example what is sometimes called 'low-key evangelism'. Various activities can be arranged in the church building with the purpose in mind to 'just get people across the threshold' and into a 'non-threatening environment'. This has come to seem natural rather than bizarre. The fact that we have lost the sense that this is strange is a sign of our adjustment to low expectations and a desire to be inoffensive. The extent to which we have adjusted is a measure of the extent to which we have been changed. Why should the world change to accommodate such people when they are willing to bend over backwards for them? If the way some people desire to 'do church' does not fit the biblical template they say, 'Let's adjust the template.' The desire to be accepted and the need to appear relevant may turn the church in a wrong direction. Let us remember the words of Paul, *'For the message of the cross is foolishness to those who are perishing, but to us who are being saved it is the power of God'* (1 Cor. 1:18).

If the business of the church is preaching the Word of God then some churches are facing bankruptcy! Although its detractors would say that preaching creates ineptitude and passivity I would contend that, where it has existed, the historical dominance of preaching has been a benefit rather than a deficit.

Is preaching disappearing? It has certainly moved to the periphery and other things are beginning to take its place at the centre. We must do all we can to halt this decline. The demise of preaching is part of a wider issue, namely, the crisis of confidence in biblical wisdom, its sufficiency and efficacy. The writer to the Hebrews should put our view of God's Word in perspective: *'For the word of God is living and active. Sharper than any double-edged sword, it penetrates even to dividing soul and spirit, joints and marrow; it judges the thoughts and attitudes of the heart'* (Heb. 4:12).

Paul tells us tells us that '...*faith comes from hearing the message...*' (Rom. 10:17). We would do well to remember that there is a message that must be told in a method ordained by God for that purpose. Paul's instruction to Timothy applies to us and has not been rescinded: '*Preach the Word; be prepared in season and out of season...*' (2 Tim. 4:2).

We read in Nehemiah that '*the Levites...instructed the people in the Law while the people were standing there. They read from the Book of the Law of God, making it clear and giving the meaning so that the people could understand what was being read*' (Neh. 8:7–8). Their wills and emotions were engaged in this process because they listened intently with a view to carrying out the instruction of the Word and they wept, '*for all the people had been weeping as they listened to the words of the Law*' (v. 9).

God's strategy for church growth

There is much written about church growth today and it is the genuine desire of believers to see others come to faith in Christ. Many approaches are being tried to win souls but we must not set aside preaching as the primary means to accomplish that goal. Scripture is clear about what means God uses to add to the church. The gospel '*is the power of God for ... salvation*' (Rom. 1:16). It pleases him by the foolishness of preaching to save those who believe (1 Cor. 1:21). What is his programme for the church? '*Preach the word ... in season and out of season; correct reprove, rebuke, exhort, with great patience and instruction*' (2 Tim. 4:2).

The New Testament record of the early church reveals that preaching should be the heart of all church activity. Preaching was the principle strategy for the growth of the early church. That growth was measured by the dissemination of the Word of God. Thus we read in Acts, '*And the word of God kept on spreading; and the number of disciples continued to increase greatly in Jerusalem*' (Acts 6:7). Again in Acts 12:24 we read, '*The word of the Lord continued to grow and be multiplied.*' Once more in Acts 19:20, '*So the word of the Lord was growing mightily and prevailing.*' Preaching is the means that God deigns to use in growing the church. The preacher is preaching for progress. He desires to see people grow in knowledge and obedience to the Word. He desires to see the church grow in unity. He desires to see souls being saved.

The strength of a church is in its pulpit and not its programmes. Preaching was the apostolic priority and God blessed it. If we are to make progress we need to give preaching that central role in our churches. Some people are disenchanted with preaching and see it as an ineffective means of reaching people in the modern world. But preaching was always seen as foolishness! There are many manuals for church growth but I would like to turn our attention back to Acts: *'And they continued steadfastly in the apostles' doctrine and fellowship, in the breaking of bread, and in prayers'* (Acts 2:42 NKJV). We see how, in that scheme, preaching plays a primary role in the progress of God's people.

The passage under consideration closes with the words, *'Then all the people went away...to celebrate with great joy, because they now understood the words that had been made known to them'* (v. 12). God wants us to be directed by his Word. It is right that we should grieve in the light of his Word which brings conviction of sin, but we should get over it by putting things right with God. The Christian life should be marked with joy because we have much to celebrate. We celebrate forgiveness of sins and eternal security. We celebrate the constant companionship of Christ. We celebrate the counsel of his Word and the comfort of the Holy Spirit. Jesus said, *'I have come that they may have life, and have it to the full'* (John 10:10). Let us take off the masks of misery and join the joyful jubilation of the redeemed!

Questions: for discussion

1. What is God's principal strategy for church growth? See Rom. 1:16; 1 Cor. 1:16–21 and 2 Tim. 4:2.
2. Read Neh. 8:1–12. What is the attitude of the people of God to the Word of God and how do our attitudes compare /contrast with theirs?
3. What does God promise in Is. 55:10–11? What encouragement might we derive from these verses?
4. Why, in your opinion, is preaching being sidelined by so-called 'more progressive practices' in today's church?
5. List the many things that a Christian has the privilege of celebrating?
6. Do you agree with the statement that 'the strength of the church is in its pulpit and not its programmes'? What role does preaching play in

inspiring, strengthening and protecting the personnel who are active in the programmes of their church?

He beholds and holds his beloved

Bible reading: Ezra 7

Focus on...

'But the eye of their God was watching over the elders of the Jews...' (Ezra 5:5)

'This Ezra came up from Babylon. He was a teacher well versed in the Law of Moses, which the LORD, the God of Israel, had given. The king had granted him everything he asked, for the hand of the LORD his God was on him.' (Ezra 7:6)

The eyes are the organs of sight through which we apprehend reality by visual means. Our optical abilities, however good, are limited to a particular range. Our field of vision is uni-directional and our focus is restricted. We have surgical procedures and spectacles to improve impaired vision. Through scientific and technological advancement human beings have been able to create telescopes and microscopes to view realities that cannot be seen with the eyes alone. The more we examine these macro and micro realities the more we learn that we know very little about our physical world.

Our finite minds find it difficult to understand how God sees all things. It is a mystery to us. But people in this age, as in all ages, readily accept mystery. How many people understand and can explain how a television works? We could ask the same question about microwaves, mobile phones, computers and so on. So there are many things we do not understand fully and yet we accept them as real.

When we consider one of the tiniest creatures in all creation, the housefly, it is amazing to think that its field of vision extends to three hundred and sixty degrees! This is a truly enviable capacity and we can only begin to imagine what differences such ability would make to human beings. It is also humbling to realise that the despised little housefly has superior visual capacities to humans!

We live in a world of sophisticated communication systems that we take for granted. Consider a person sitting in the control room of a television studio with twelve TV screens, each one showing a different image and he directs that the image to be transmitted to viewers will come from camera number six. The police use CCTV to monitor activity on the streets of our cities to prevent and solve crime. At the push of a few buttons satellites can beam in on whatever target is desired.

Technology, therefore, has helped us to overcome some of our limitations, from rear-view mirrors in our cars that enable us to look in a westerly direction when we are driving eastwards, to satellites that transmit live television images from the other side of the world. Infrared cameras with various applications serve us in the nocturnal hours of darkness. Digital and mobile phone photography and the internet create a world of instant access to images.

God sees everything

In all of this we see that man strives for the ability of ubiquitous sight, and though his achievements are truly remarkable, they fall infinitely short of the divine capacity to see all things. The visual ability of the Lord is omni-directional and unlimited. He watches all things and sees so much that displeases him. Nothing is secret to him. Walls and shut doors do not obscure his vision. The awful depravity of this world wrings the heart of God.

But it is wonderful to think that he keeps a fond eye on his children. He observes them closely and watches over them with tender loving care. He is not a God who observes dispassionately from the control room. May that observation please him! What a wonderful thing it is for a child to behold his father's face looking at him admiringly. God is alert and watches his children intently. He has his eye on us because we belong to him and he is interested in us. '...*He who watches over you will not slumber; indeed, he who watches over Israel will neither slumber nor sleep. The LORD watches over you...*' (Ps. 121:3b-4a). God is never caught unawares. Nothing happens to him unexpectedly because he has foresight of all things. We may inadvertently find ourselves in difficult circumstances but God is in control and he is concerned and compassionate. He keeps an eye on his children to protect and preserve them.

He longs to bless and scans the globe to find those who are dedicated to him: *'For the eyes of the LORD range throughout the earth to strengthen those whose hearts are fully committed to him'* (2 Chron. 16:9). Many Scriptures attest to the truth that God oversees those who trust in him. Psalm 33:18 says, *'But the eyes of the LORD are on those who fear him, on those whose hope is in his unfailing love.'* In the New Testament Peter affirms the same truth: *'For the eyes of the Lord are on the righteous'* (1 Pet. 3:12). Those who are deemed to be righteous are those who are trusting in that unfailing love demonstrated at Calvary.

May we never give God cause to look away from us by grieving him! The Lord told the people of Israel through the prophet Isaiah that he would avert his loving gaze from them because of their wickedness: 'When you spread out your hands in prayer, I will hide my eyes from you; even if you offer many prayers, I will not listen. Your hands are full of blood…' (Is. 1:15). He has set the eyes of his affection on us. When he surveys the earth in search of those who are committed to him will he find us in that place of loyal love? May our lives be pleasing in his eyes so that he can dispense the blessing he desires!

The Lord had sent the people of Israel into captivity in Babylon for their habitual and flagrant violations of his revealed will for them. They were disobedient and spurned the grace extended to them. Yet he kept his eyes on them until they were ready to be directed by his loving counsel. Thus we read in Jeremiah, 'This is what the LORD, the God of Israel, says: "Like these good figs, I regard as good the exiles from Judah, whom I sent away from this place to the land of the Babylonians. My eyes will watch over them for their good, and I will bring them back to this land. I will build them up and not tear them down; I will plant them and not uproot them. I will give them a heart to know me, that I am the LORD. They will be my people, and I will be their God, for they will return to me with all their heart."' (Jer. 24:5–7). The Lord watched for that moment of repentance, ready to restore and reward those who responded to his watchful care. Let us never forget that the Lord beholds his beloved.

The hand of God

Now we direct our attention to that verse in chapter seven of Ezra: 'This Ezra came up from Babylon. He was a teacher well versed in the Law of Moses, which the LORD, the God of Israel, had given. The king had granted him everything he asked, for the hand of the LORD his God was on him' (v. 6). The phrase 'for the hand of the LORD his God was on him' is a refrain that is repeated with minor variations in other places in the book of Ezra. For example, chapter seven verse nine says 'for the gracious hand of his God was on him' and again in chapter eight verse eighteen '...the gracious hand of our God was on us.' It is always instructive to look at the phrases that are repeated in a portion of Scripture as they often indicate an important theme. It is as if the Holy Spirit is putting a particular emphasis on the issue.

But what does it mean to have the gracious hand of God upon an individual or a people? It is a truly awesome thought to contemplate that the hand of the Almighty might be involved in our affairs on earth. It is not, in fact, that his hand is involved in *our* affairs; rather, he is operative in *his* concerns and we may be instrumental in those purposes. This phrase *'for the hand of the LORD his God was on him'* speaks of the reality that God protects his people and provides for them. It also speaks of the certainty that he promotes his purposes through his people.

The hand of God speaks of his almighty power. He is omnipotent. Isaiah reminds us of the awesome majesty of God, *'Who has measured the waters in the hollow of his hand, or with the breadth of his hand marked off the heavens? Who has held the dust of the earth in a basket, or weighed the mountains on the scales and the hills in a balance?'* (Is. 40:12). This is a vivid picture of the consummate ease with which the almighty God created the universe. When we consider this it is astounding that such a God takes a personal interest in his people. He is the same God who says to his people, *'See, I have engraved you on the palms of my hands'* (Is. 49:16).

His power has not diminished. There is reproof in the Lord's rhetorical question to Moses, *'Is the LORD's arm too short?'* (Num. 11:23). God directs that question to all his people as he did in the time of Jeremiah: *'I am the LORD, the God of all mankind. Is anything too hard for me?'* (Jer. 32:27). Given the way the question is put it would be impossible to answer anything other than 'certainly not!' That is the answer that faith demands.

He is the creator and the one who sustains all life as Job tells us: *'In his hand is the life of every creature and the breath of all mankind'* (Job 12:10).

The hand of God is an anthropomorphic term for the creative power and providential care of God. His people are the beneficiaries of his particular bountiful benefaction. It is also a term that relates to the power of God to punish. God is merciful and mighty but he is also perfectly holy and just. A day of judgement is coming when he shall judge the living and the dead. That will be a glorious day for those whose sins are covered by the precious blood of the Saviour, the Lord Jesus Christ. But for those outside the covenant of that blood it will be a terrible day because it will be the beginning of conscious torment and eternal separation from God. Thus the writer to the Hebrews reminds us, *'It is a dreadful thing to fall into the hands of the living God'* (Heb. 10:31).

In an earlier chapter, 'Union, Uniformity, Unity', we considered how effective true unity may be in progressing the aims of the Almighty. We remarked then that such unity is to be highly prized indeed. As we consider the hand of God on these people we must be aware that it was his hand that caused unity to prevail. Before ever the remnant embarked on the project of returning and rebuilding, God took the initiative, stirred their hearts and gave them that heavenly concord of purpose. So we read, *'Also in Judah the hand of God was on the people to give them unity of mind to carry out what the king and his officials had ordered, following the word of the LORD'* (2 Chron. 30:12).

Above all, the phrase *'the hand of God'* speaks of his unquestionable authority and unlimited ability. We are reminded in the book of Daniel, *'He does as he pleases with the powers of heaven and the peoples of the earth. No one can hold back his hand or say to him: "What have you done?"'* (Dan. 4:35). Knowing that our God is such a God ought to instil security and confidence in our hearts. Remember the words of Jesus, *'I give them eternal life, and they shall never perish; no one can snatch them out of my hand'* (John 10:28). Let us never forget that it is this God who holds and beholds his beloved.

Questions: for discussion

1. See Ps. 121:3b-4a; 2 Chron. 16:9; Ps. 33:18; 1 Pet. 3:12. Nothing is

hidden from God. Do you find this thought comforting or disturbing? Why?

2. What does the phrase *'the hand of God'* mean?

3. According to Is. 1:15 our prayers may be ineffective in certain circumstances. Apart from the blood-stained hands that this verse speaks of, what other things grieve the Lord? See Ex. 20:1–17.

4. Consider how God protected his people throughout Old Testament times and how he provided for them so that he could ultimately see his purposes progressed in and through his people. In what way is God still providing for and protecting his people in accordance with a specific plan? How have you (individually and as a church) known his provision, protection and purposes being brought to fruition?

5. The phrase *'the hand of God'* speaks of the creative power and providential care of God. But Heb. 10:31 draws attention to another understanding of the phrase. What does this verse tell us about 'the hand of God'?

6. Has God's authority and ability diminished in an increasingly secular world? See Num. 11:23; Jer. 32:27; Dan. 4:35.

A prepared person

Bible reading: Ezra 7

Focus on…

'For Ezra had prepared his heart to seek the Law of the Lord, and to do it, and to teach statutes and ordinances in Israel.' (Ezra 7:10 NKJV)

Ezra was a Jew who was brought up in the kingdom of Persia. As such he was born and raised a displaced person and ministered in the second half of the fifth century BC. He was a trusted official who occupied an important position in the court of the Emperor of Persia (Artaxerxes) as a confidante. He had never seen Jerusalem and lived in an alien and pagan atmosphere. Yet he is a man who is remembered as a significant individual in the sweep of spiritual posterity. His influence on the kingdom of God in that period and afterwards is significant. People used to think of him as a second Moses because of the great revival of God's work that happened under him. At this particular point (Ezra 7:10) he has just returned to Jerusalem, leading a great company of Jews to build again in that place.

Why should we turn back to this man to seek to learn something from him? What is the key to understanding his usefulness in the hands of God? Can we learn from him? What made him so useful not only in his day but after his day? It is instructive for us to note that although brought up in a polytheistic and foreign environment, he was obviously a man who came to know the God of Israel. It is edifying to examine Ezra and consider what God can accomplish through just one man. It is important to ask not only what made Ezra effective but also what it is that can make us usable. It is not that we meet certain terms and conditions and thereby qualify to invoke the power of God to enable us to accomplish wonderful things. But it is instructive to investigate those whom God deigns to use with a view to discovering some principles that promote effectiveness.

In that same period of Old Testament history we meet with others like him who left a mark on their generation, such as Daniel (100 years before Ezra), Queen Esther, and the man who came after Ezra, Nehemiah. Just individuals, yet God graciously condescended to employ these people to accomplish his purposes.

As believers we ought to want our lives to be instrumental in accomplishing God's glorious plans in our generation. We don't want to waste our lives by living aimlessly. But how can we be useful to God? Is there a clue in Scripture to this secret that we might learn it? It was Jim Elliot who said, *'Only one life, 'twill soon be passed, only what's done for Christ will last.'* If we have a heavenly perspective about this temporal world these words should impress us very deeply. Ezra was a man who found the key to being useful. What made him eligible for service in the kingdom? What made him the man that he was and what lessons can we extrapolate and emulate to make us the people we should be?

Profile of a preacher

Consider the way this verse begins: *'For Ezra had prepared his heart…'* At that point he had just come up to Jerusalem, which was a long journey from Persia. But this first part of the verse takes us back to another, earlier point in his life. Evidently there was a time when Ezra made an important decision. He *'had prepared his heart'*. If he had not come to that point would we ever have heard of him? The name Ezra may never have come down to us over twenty-five centuries later. From that moment on he knew where he was going. There may have been days of doubt but he had determined in his heart to prepare himself for usefulness. He was not going to live aimlessly. He was going in a certain direction. He had decided that issue. He may have had problems but his priorities from that moment on had been sorted out. The chief aim of his life had been determined. There was a point where this man realised that he had only one life, that God had given it to him, and that his life was not his own to live.

He realised then what the apostle Paul sought to convey to the Corinthian church and, indeed what the Holy Spirit is seeking to convey to us: *'…do you not know… you are not your own?'* (1 Cor. 6:19). Or equally: *'For you were bought at a price; therefore glorify God in your body and in your spirit, which are God's'* (1 Cor. 6:20 NKJV). Ezra could very well have expressed himself in words such as these. He is determined that he will live his life to the glory of God and earnestly pursues that goal.

Heart religion

Much the same thing is said in the opening chapter of the book of Daniel. Daniel was a stranger in Babylon who realised that he had to sort out his priorities. The crunch came one day when Daniel saw that unless he made a decision about how he would live, he would be overwhelmed by the prevailing culture. Nebuchadnezzar was trying to spiritually subjugate him and if he had not made a crucial decision he would have lost his identity as one of God's people. He would have become like everybody else. However we read, *'But Daniel purposed in his heart that he would not defile himself with the portion of the king's delicacies, nor with the wine which he drank; therefore he requested of the chief of the eunuchs that he might not defile himself'* (Dan. 1:8 NKJV). That was a very important moment in Daniel's life. What has been previously stated about Ezra may equally be said about Daniel. That is, we would never have heard of him unless he had come to that point in his life where he *'purposed in his heart.'* So it was that Ezra set his heart on God and the things of eternity.

William Carey, the Baptist missionary at the end of the eighteenth century, was one day at his work as a cobbler in Northampton when someone who visited him said, 'I see that you are a cobbler.' 'No', said Carey, 'My business is the kingdom of God but I'm doing this to pay the expenses.' He was really saying that the thing his heart was set on was the kingdom of God, the good of souls in India! This is what motivated him and moved him. And the same is true of Ezra. The thing that constrained him was not a compelling ambition to lead the community of God's people to return to the homeland. Rather it was, initially at least, a longing to please God.

We will make nothing of our lives unless we come to that point where our primary aspiration is a yearning after God. This issue needs to be settled. Where are we going? Are we determined in our hearts? As Christians we know the grace of God. We know how Jesus died for us on the cross. We know these things, we believe and rejoice in them! Now knowing that, do we know what our lives are going to be about? Do we know our direction? There are many people today who are wandering aimlessly, even as Christians, through life. They are not quite sure what it is all about and where they are going.

Now this man Ezra, at a certain point, decided he would be God's man and that he would seek God's will and do it. That is the place to begin! *'For Ezra had prepared his heart.'* How much heart religion do we really have today? How much of our heart is in our profession? How much in our inner hearts do we deal with God? What does God see in us today as he looks at us? Does he see people who have decided and who have their priorities clear? Unless our hearts are settled in this issue, unless our priorities are clear our lives will drift by aimlessly.

Preparation: a prelude or prerequisite?

'This Ezra came up from Babylon. He was a teacher well versed in the Law of Moses, which the LORD, the God of Israel, had given. The king had granted him everything he asked, for the hand of the LORD his God was on him' (Ezra 7:6).

Preparation for the work of God is not merely a preliminary duty to be discharged and dispensed with as soon as possible. Before Ezra ever stood on the threshold of a great revival he knelt before his God in preparation for the work to which he would be commissioned. This aspect of ministry in the Word of God must never be seen merely as a prelude to the real work of preaching and teaching. It is rather a prerequisite condition of one's commissioning. He had studied the law of the Lord diligently. The apostle Paul instructed Timothy, *'Do your best to present yourself to God as one approved, a workman who does not need to be ashamed and who correctly handles the word of truth'* (2 Tim. 2:15). Ezra was a *'ready scribe'* and as such he had done what Paul counselled Timothy to do. He had done his best and presented himself before God as a competent minister in the Word.

That process of preparation was thorough and complete and so he was in a fit state to serve his God. Undoubtedly the process began with a willingness to work for God. Whatever the inclination of his heart he resolved to do all that he could to make himself fit for use. The statement that he was a *'ready scribe'* indicates that he was fit for immediate use. He was about to accomplish great things for God because he was prepared before the time of opportunity arrived. When the time came for use he was ready.

Ezra was *'a teacher well versed in the Law of Moses'* (Ezra 7:6). The Authorised Version says *'...he was a ready scribe in the law of Moses...'* (Ezra 7:6) and in Nehemiah he is frequently called a scribe. The word 'scribe' can have different meanings in different contexts, much the same as 'secretary' can mean a government minister (Secretary of State) or an office administrator employed to assist with correspondence, records, making appointments, etc. The primary function of a scribe was to make copies of the Scripture. The office involved classifying and teaching the precepts of the law and meticulously counting each letter of Old Testament writing. This kind of attention to detail was a legitimate function, at the time of Ezra, in a religion of law and precepts. However, the scribes began to add a record of rabbinical decisions on issues relating to ritual (*Halachoth*). This new system became the prevailing standard of moral behaviour (*Mishna*). The Hebrew sacred legends (*Gemara*) together with the *Mishna* formed the *Talmud*. To this was added the explanatory writings on the Old Testament (*Midrashim*) together with conclusions argued from these (*Hagada*). Finally, mystical interpretations not based on the obvious meaning of a text and not grounded in grammatical and lexical scholarship (*the Kabbala*) came to form part of the contribution of the scribes to the Judaic system of beliefs.

All of this meant that four centuries after Ezra, in the New Testament period at the time of Jesus' incarnate earthly ministry, this group of scholars had lost any real sense of true spirituality and had become an elite and esoteric group. Their writings, which had been superimposed upon Scripture, were deemed to be orthodox but they effectively obscured God's Word.

However, during the time of the monarchy of the united kingdom (Israel in the north and Judah in the south) a scribe was a royal secretary. But in the later period of the divided kingdom the occupation of the scribes had changed and they had become interpreters of the law. Their business was to show its application to all the changing circumstances of life. They mediated the will and wisdom of God. Whereas the prophets received new revelations, the scribes explained and applied the old in the contemporary context. Thus to say that Ezra was a *'ready scribe'* means that he was an expert in the exposition and application of the law of Moses.

So here was a man who was ready, a man who was prepared. Ezra was not a scribe like those at the time of Jesus because he was not merely an expert in knowledge. His skill was not confined to the subject of knowing chapter and verse. Rather his expertise was related to experience. His knowledge was more than familiarity with the nuances and scholarly interpretations of textual analysis. His was an awareness of the implications and application of the law. He had an intimacy with its author and realised its efficacious and edifying value. He had no desire to be involved in merely imparting information. He desired to see God's people come under the transformational power of God's counsel. No doubt his understanding of the subject matter was great, but that understanding extended to knowing its author, the Lord himself. So it was not just that he was well informed and knowledgeable about the law; rather, that he was well acquainted with the Lord. It is only such people who will ever be of any use to God. So our preparation to minister in the Word must not be confined to an academic approach to a branch of knowledge (theology). The first duty of all those who want to teach the Word of God is to get to know God himself. So it is not just that Ezra was educated in the law in the sense that his mental powers and stock of knowledge meant that he was equipped to deliver systematic instruction. Rather, his character was developed in accordance with that law and that is the penultimate aim of spiritual education. The ultimate aim, of course, is the glory of God. We are models of a message that points to the Master. So before ever he was a teacher he was teachable.

Ezra was not the only one who prepared. We read in the first chapter of this book, *'Then the family heads of Judah and Benjamin, and the priests and Levites—everyone whose heart God had moved—prepared to go up and build the house of the LORD in Jerusalem'* (Ezra 1:5). He preached to a prepared people. All of God's people have a responsibility to prepare themselves for worship, witness and work.

God prepares
The Master is our mentor and we know from Scripture that he prepares:

'No eye has seen, no ear has heard, no mind has conceived what God has prepared for those who love him' (1 Cor. 2:9). On one occasion Jesus told his disciples, 'I am going there to prepare a place for you' (John 14:2). This is also stated by the writer to the Hebrews, '…God is not ashamed to be called their God, for he has prepared a city for them' (Heb. 11:16). It is an extraordinary thought but one worthy of attention that God prepares work for us to do. Paul told the Ephesians, 'For we are God's workmanship, created in Christ Jesus to do good works, which God prepared in advance for us to do' (Eph. 2:10). Parents sometimes prepare work for their children in order to train them or get them started on some task. Our heavenly father does this for us.

We are to be prepared

The child of God must be in a state of readiness to give an account of his faith. This is the privilege and duty of all those who belong to him and ought to be taken seriously. There is no excuse for the Christian who cannot explain his faith. That does not mean one has to be a theologian but it does mean one has to be prepared to testify on behalf of Jesus. Peter makes this quite clear to a people who were suffering because of their faith. In that context it is more than practical advice for Christian living. It is a call to courageously communicate our faith in a world that is hostile to the gospel: 'But in your hearts set apart Christ as Lord. Always be prepared to give an answer to everyone who asks you to give the reason for the hope that you have. But do this with gentleness and respect' (1 Pet. 3:15).

If we wish to be useful instruments in the hands of God and serve his noble purposes we need to be in a prepared condition. In Paul's second letter to Timothy he uses a household illustration to convey the necessity of preparation for service: 'In a large house there are articles not only of gold and silver, but also of wood and clay; some are for noble purposes and some for ignoble. If a man cleanses himself from the latter, he will be an instrument for noble purposes, made holy, useful to the Master and prepared to do any good work' (2 Tim. 2:20–21). Every preacher must be prepared, whether it is fashionable or not, to proclaim the truth without fear or favour. It is not what is in vogue that is important but the verity of God's Word. Thus Paul says to Timothy, 'Preach the Word; be prepared in season and out of season; correct, rebuke and encourage—with great patience and careful instruction' (2 Tim. 4:2).

Questions: for discussion

1. In what area of one's life should preparation for service to God begin?
2. How does 1 Cor. 6:19–20 motivate us to serve God wholeheartedly?
3. What do we learn about God from the following verses 1 Cor. 2:9; John 14:2; Heb. 11:16; Eph. 2:10?
4. What does 2 Tim. 2:21 teach us about the necessity of preparation for service to God?
5. Why should we look back to Ezra? What can we learn from him? What is the key to understanding his usefulness in the hands of God? See Ezra 7:10.
6. Ezra was a scribe. In what way(s) was he different from the scribes encountered by Christ in the New Testament accounts?

The study of Scripture

Bible reading: Ezra 7

Focus on...

'For Ezra had prepared his heart to seek the Law of the Lord, and to do it, and to teach statutes and ordinances in Israel.' (Ezra 7:10 NKJV)

We have already considered how Ezra had arrived at a point in his life where he 'prepared his heart.' There is no secret combination code to unlock the vault of heaven's blessing, but Ezra provides an example we would do well to emulate. His vital preparation of heart had to begin somewhere, and the exhortation inherent through his example is that we ought to prepare our hearts as seedbeds for God's purposes. But what, specifically, did he decide? What was it that Ezra set his heart on and how did he prepare for service?

He was probably a busy man as a court official and as a scribe among the Jews of Persia. Yet he was preparing for God to use him in the future. His preparation led him 'to seek the Law of the Lord' and this is exemplary for God's people in any generation.

An incomparable treasure

He did not have a New Testament and had only part of the Old Testament but he immersed himself in it. It is important to observe that he didn't just set himself an academic, intellectual exercise. From the outset it was something much more to him. He believed that this Word that God had given to his people was an incomparable treasure and that there was nothing in Persia to equate with it. Ezra believed that the Almighty God had spoken and made known his purposes and promises through the parchments and manuscripts available, and these became precious to him.

From the beginning he put himself under the authority of this Word of

God. He set himself the task of mastering Scripture and so he got to grips with the eternal and unchanging truths of God. It might be more accurate to say that he allowed the Word to master him, to search him out and teach him. In spite of his busy schedule he took time to familiarise himself with that Word which was precious to him. It was that knowledge of God's Word which contributed significantly to him becoming a useful instrument in God's grand scheme.

Paul said to Timothy, 'From childhood you have known the Holy Scriptures, which are able to make you wise for salvation through faith which is in Christ Jesus' (2 Tim. 3:15). He also instructed him not to be smug about such wonderful knowledge but to 'study to shew thyself approved unto God a workman that needeth not to be ashamed, rightly dividing the word of truth' (2 Tim. 2:15, AV). Every believer is exhorted to be diligent in this matter. It is not, necessarily, about being biblical scholars but it is about allowing the Word of God to dwell richly in our hearts. I wonder how many would be 'ashamed' precisely because they have neglected to study Scripture? Some Christians today don't bother attending meetings where the Word of God is faithfully expounded, particularly on Sunday evenings and mid-week Bible study times. There is an apathy or carelessness about Scripture, and for some there is even a disregard for the practical implications of its teaching in the reality of their lives. Many believers have an 'a la carte' approach to Scripture as if it were a menu from which they can select what pleases them and leave what does not suit! There is a shallow understanding of the deep things of God, which can be attributed to the neglect of his Word.

Guided and governed by God

Here we see that Ezra, just like Timothy, came to be guided and governed by God's Word. That is the way he begins to prepare himself for his future life. He is determined to avoid living aimlessly by allowing himself to be directed by Scripture. We need to ask ourselves: is that true of us? Are we a people like that? Do we see ourselves as under the authority of God's Word? Do we belong to a church where the Word of God is consistently and faithfully preached? We should! Every Christian should do everything in his power to be in a situation where he is fed with the milk and meat of the

Word of God. It is our business to permit this Word of God to permeate our thinking and to mould and master us! Are we in that sort of situation? Do we read and study our Bibles? Not so that we can know more than others do but so that his Word can shape our attitude and actions!

I wonder if the next generation will look back on this age as a period when people were renowned for zeal for the Word of God? We have commentaries, concordances, Bible dictionaries and all sorts of studies and helps (including electronic aids such as computer software) but I wonder if we are a people who really get down to our Bibles? Do we allow the Scripture to control us?

Ezra, with as much of the Scripture as he had available to him, allowed the Word of God to master him. Most of us know the verse, *'Your word is a lamp to my feet and a light to my path'* (Ps. 119:105 NKJV). But how much do we rely on the illumination of this lamp in our experience? We live in a dark world where light is needed, but do we tend to rely more on our senses and intellect and the counsel of friends, even godless counsel, rather than on the pure Word of God? *'Your word I have hidden in my heart, that I might not sin against you!'* (Ps. 119:11 NKJV). How much of the Word have we hidden in our hearts? Often there is more of the world than the Word in our hearts! We know we should treasure the Word in our hearts but there seems to be a crisis of confidence in the efficacious nature of Scripture.

It is a practice that has fallen out of fashion to memorise Scripture. Of course it may also be said that some have stored it in their heads. Ps. 119:11 does not say, *'Your word I have hidden in my HEAD, that I might not sin against you!'* The Word is meant to permeate every area of our lives. We are meant to treasure it and store it in the place where our affections are ruled (i.e. our hearts). Some Christians would be helpful members of a biblical knowledge quiz team, yet they are not the kind of people to whom any responsibility can be delegated because their hearts have not assimilated their head knowledge. It is only when that process of assimilation has taken place that Scripture is transformational.

Apathy rooted in ignorance

Apathy about the Word of God is rooted in ignorance of the vital importance of its role in equipping his people to safeguard and strengthen the strategic purposes of God. Paul told the Ephesians to '...*take the helmet of salvation, and the sword of the Spirit, which is the word of God*' (Eph. 6:17). The writer to the Hebrews says, '*For the word of God is living and powerful, and sharper than any two-edged sword, piercing even to the division of soul and spirit, and of joints and marrow, and is a discerner of the thoughts and intents of the heart*' (Heb. 4:12 NKJV). Sadly, many have a lack of awareness or even a reckless disregard of the danger in letting the authoritative role of Scripture slip into abeyance.

How to study Scripture

Ezra found the key to a life of usefulness for God in coming to a place where he understood the mind of God through His Word. Furthermore, he allowed that Word to mould and manage him and in so doing became a useful instrument in God's hands. How can we follow his example by more effectively engaging in the practical discipline of biblical study? Solomon counsels us to seek out the treasures of God's Word. In Proverbs 2:1–5 we read, '*My son, if you accept my words and store up my commands within you, turning your ear to wisdom and applying your heart to understanding, and if you call out for insight and cry aloud for understanding, and if you look for it as for silver and search for it as for hidden treasure, then you will understand the fear of the LORD and find the knowledge of God.*' The study of Scripture begins with a yearning for the things of God. Once that desire to study Scripture is stimulated it needs to be steered along a meaningful course. Wanting to make that commitment, however, is the first step in commencing a work that will be exceptionally profitable (2 Tim. 3:16).

Spiritual Discernment

The Bible is not just a historical or literary textbook and should not, therefore, be approached only in an academic manner without giving due heed to its essential nature as the living Word of the Almighty God. The apostle Paul understood this truth and sought to communicate it to the Corinthian church when he said, '*The man without the Spirit does not accept the things that come from the Spirit of God, for they are foolishness to him, and he cannot understand them, because they are spiritually discerned'* (1 Cor. 2:14). Only those who have been born again of the Spirit of God can discern spiritual matters. The unregenerate are unable to understand the true meaning and fullest significance of God's Word. It is only when he graciously calls those whom he has chosen in Christ, and they in turn are irresistibly drawn by that grace, that the words of eternal life take on their true significance. If one is thinking of pursuing a formal course of biblical study there are many things to be considered, but the pre-eminent consideration must be to have soundly converted Christian teachers. A man may have impressive academic credentials, but if he is not born again his spiritual perspective will be seriously flawed and ultimately it will be futile to submit oneself to the auspices of such a person.

As it is God's holy Word that is under investigation a prayerful approach is appropriate when handling the eternal words of life! If the task seems a little daunting one may take encouragement from James who says, *'If any of you lacks wisdom, he should ask God, who gives generously'* (James 1:5). Any approach to the study of the Bible that does not begin with prayer is, therefore, defective. Ultimately the Holy Spirit is our tutor. Imagine a man who is an author and he has written something that his child does not understand. It is only natural for the child to ask the father to explain, and any decent father will patiently and diligently set about communicating the meaning in language that is comprehensible to his child. Will your heavenly father do any less for you?

Motivation

Why should we want to study the Bible? Scripture asserts, 'In the past God spoke to our forefathers through the prophets at many times and in various ways, but in these last days he has spoken to us by his Son...' (Heb. 1:1–2). We should, therefore, desire to hear and understand what he has to say. What he has said is recorded in the Bible. Paul tells Timothy, 'All scripture is God-breathed and is useful for teaching, rebuking, correcting and training in righteousness, so that the man of God may be thoroughly equipped for every good work' (2 Tim. 3:16–17). We ought to want to study Scripture in order that our appreciation of its meaning may be applied in our daily experience. We should read it with an intense level of appreciation and curiosity as if it were the last will and testament of a benevolent benefactor who has named us as beneficiaries and bequeathed to us vast wealth. We should read it as a fiancée would read the letters of her beloved.

The following quotation is a comprehensive and succinct statement that summarises why we should feel impelled to explore the Scriptures:

'The Bible contains the mind of God, the state of man, the way of salvation, the doom of sinners, and the happiness of believers. Its doctrines are holy, its precepts are binding, its histories are true, and its decisions are immutable. Read it to be wise, believe it to be safe, and practise it to be holy. It contains light to direct you, food to support you, and comfort to cheer you.

It is the traveller's map, the pilgrim's staff, the pilot's compass, the soldier's sword and the Christian's charter. Here Paradise is restored, Heaven opened, and the gates of hell disclosed.

Christ is its grand subject, our good the design, and the glory of God its end. It should fill the memory, rule the heart, and guide the feet. Read it slowly, frequently, and prayerfully. It is a mine of wealth, a paradise of glory, and a river of pleasure. It is given you in life, will be opened at the judgement, and be remembered forever. It involves the highest responsibility, will reward the greatest labour, and will condemn all who trifle with its sacred contents.'[1]

Investigation

Most of us depend on the scholarship of others to help in the study of Scripture. However, it is important to remember that it is the Bible that has to be the centre of our investigation. It is far too easy to forget this and to begin to rely too much on what other people have written about the Bible. In spite of the fact that we can derive enormous benefit from the writings of others concerning this book, we must not neglect to consult the original subject, the inspired Word itself. It is important to consult good books, commentaries, expository material and Bible dictionaries, as well as theological and historical works. Nevertheless we have something to learn from the Bereans whom we read about in Acts. They tested the truth of Paul's claims by searching the Scriptures for themselves in order to verify the validity of his claims. A number of them found that there was sufficient evidence to warrant a verdict of proven and yielded to its consequential demand for faith (Acts 17:10–12).

A systematic approach to the study of the Bible will be most advantageous and this will necessitate a thorough investigation of whatever portion of Scripture is being considered. The central question to be addressed at this stage is: what is the intended meaning and purpose of the passage? Attention must be paid to the text and context and we should be aware that 'context' has three dimensions. They are the immediate, wider and widest contexts. Remember that a verse fits into a chapter, a chapter fits into a book, a book fits into a genre and they all fit together as a whole. Many cults have been founded on misinterpretation and misrepresentation of texts taken out of context. At a simple level we could say that the Bible says *'there is no God'* (Ps. 14:1; 53:1). That is a true statement; the Bible does say *'there is no God'*, but the immediate context reveals that it is it not a true meaning because it is *'the fool'* who says this in his heart. We may extrapolate from this the necessity to be careful about context. The words of Job's 'comforters', Bildad, Eliphaz and Zophar, need to be taken in context too. Although they form part of Scripture their perception and counsel serve as a foil to illustrate the innocence of Job. The fact that some terrible things happen in the Bible does not mean that God approves of such things. They are recorded to demonstrate the total depravity of man. Care is needed in discerning context.

As well as observing the surface meaning of the text one should also examine the background and the particular genre of the passage. Whether it is poetic, historic or prophetic is important in the process of determining the meaning. This approach will require some background reading and, therefore, access to good resources. Bible study is a process of analysis and synthesis under the illuminating influence of the Holy Spirit. It is important to know where a passage fits in and how it relates to other sections of the Word. This synthesis takes time to develop and is helped greatly by a systematic, regular and consistent approach to reading Scripture. As we interrogate Scripture we will find that it is a book that actually interrogates us! It is a humbling, though not humiliating, experience to learn that although we are not worthless in the eyes of God we are unworthy of his grace and favour. A Bible that is not smudged with tears has never been read properly.

Let us take account of the background, literary style and structure of the text. Let us observe the main theme and identify the purpose of the passage. Allow Scripture to interpret Scripture by using a concordance and checking the cross-referencing chain of your Bible. Consult a good systematic theology and check your work against reliable commentaries. If you do not command a working knowledge of Hebrew and Greek you can still study the meanings of biblical words in their original languages by using an expository dictionary and interlinear aid. There is an input/output ratio in study of any kind whereby the more effort you make the greater will be the reward. We must remember, however, that the chief aim of biblical studies is to produce transformed lives that glorify God.

After the resurrection, when Jesus met the two disciples on the road to Emmaus he conducted a Bible study that must have been astonishing for Cleopas and the other disciple. In Luke 24:27 we read, *'And beginning with Moses and all the Prophets, he explained to them what was said in all the Scriptures concerning himself.'* Christ is the golden thread in all the Scriptures, both Old and New Testaments. He is in the Old Testament in type and shadow. He is central to the plot as the promise of prophecy. If we interrogate the text with the question 'how does this relate to Christ?' it will prove to be a very profitable exercise.

Interrogate the Word by asking who, what, where, when, why and how? One question that I always (reverently) ask of a passage of Scripture in order to get at the application of the text is 'so what?' Christ was born in Bethlehem, 'so what?' God promised it would be so and God keeps his promises and we can trust him to do so. Christ Jesus came into the world to save sinners, 'so what?' Do you trust his promises? God promises heaven to those in Christ and hell to those outside Christ. Which will be your final destination?

Questions: for discussion

1. Ezra saw the Word of God as an incomparable treasure. How do we view Scripture? See Ps. 119:11; Eph. 6:17 and Heb. 4:12.
2. How much do we rely on the Word of God to guide and govern our lives? See Ps. 119:105. In what areas is God's government and guidance most needed?
3. Paul's advice to Timothy in 2 Tim. 2:15 also applies to us. How

seriously do we take this instruction? List some ways that would help us to fulfil this obligation and enjoy the privilege of Bible study.
4. What role does the Holy Spirit play in Bible study?
5. How can Scripture be interrogated? What is the chief aim of biblical studies?
6. Where can you see Jesus in the Old Testament?

Footnote

1   Quoted from *Gideons International New Testament, Psalms and Proverbs,* Thomas Nelson Inc., 1985.

Practice and preaching

Bible reading: Ezra 7

Focus on…

'For Ezra had prepared his heart to seek the Law of the Lord, and to do it, and to teach statutes and ordinances in Israel.' (Ezra 7:10 NKJV)

Preaching that persuades

Why had Ezra *'prepared his heart to seek the Law of the Lord'*? It was not to develop cerebral powers and intellectual faculties, but as the verse tells us, his first priority was *'to do it'*. In other words he was determined to put it into practice. Before ever the Word of God is preached it must be practised. He studied the law of the Lord in order that his conduct might come to reflect that knowledge. It wasn't just something abstract and theoretical in his thinking. Nor was it something just private and personal.

The people who knew him (family, fellow Jews and the pagans around him in the court of Persia) came to know that here was a life that was directed by the law of God. In his life godly attitudes and behaviour animated the Scriptures. In other words, he was a vivid and living illustration of the reality of God through incarnational living. We do well to remember that we are the only Bibles many people will ever read! His whole life became an outworking of the principles that he found in the Word of God. Now that is the way we should study our Bibles. That is the way we should approach Scripture. That too is the way we should come to church and listen to the exhortation of the Word. We shouldn't just be sermon tasters who critique performances in accordance with the criteria for public speaking and oratory. Too often we compare preachers with preachers and discuss the merits and demerits of one style against another. The important thing is not what we think of the sermon but what we do about it!

God speaks through his Word and reveals his mind and will regarding what he wants us to be. Our business, therefore, as we read the Word of God and listen to it preached is to allow that Word to permeate our thinking in such a way that our lives are influenced by that Word. Otherwise our knowledge of the Scriptures will be a sheer mockery. We mock God when we know the Word and don't practise it: *'Do not merely listen to the word, and so deceive yourselves. Do what it says'* (James 1:22). What use is this glorious teaching if it doesn't change us and in so doing bring glory to God? Paul says that we are *'... being transformed into his likeness with ever-increasing glory...'* (2 Cor. 3:18). That activity of the Holy Spirit occurs when the Scriptures shape us. Thus our conduct will be delivered from unreality when we learn from the Word of God how to live.

Go forth and tell

Firstly, Ezra had prepared his heart in the way a farmer cultivates the soil making it ready to receive the seed. This he understood as the foremost step in being instrumental in God's service. Secondly, he devoted himself to knowing the Word of God intimately. Thirdly, he sought to live out that Word in every part of his life (private and public) and in so doing had credibility and authority. Fourthly, he realised that he had a responsibility to people around him and that this great truth was to be shared with others. He not only *'prepared his heart to study the law of the Lord and to do it'*, but now, having done that (and only then) he was able *'to teach statutes and ordinances in Israel.'*

Others need to know God's revealed mind. His age, like ours, was an age of falsehood. He recognised that in a pagan culture (with its multiplicity of gods) people needed above everything else to hear the truth of God. This is the same instinct that David had when he prayed, *'Create in me a clean heart, O God, and renew a steadfast spirit within me. Do not cast me away from Your presence, and do not take Your Holy Spirit from me. Restore to me the joy of Your salvation, and uphold me by Your generous Spirit. Then I will teach transgressors Your ways, and sinners shall be converted to You'* (Ps. 51:10–13 NKJV).

This is the order in which Ezra sorted things and if we want to be useful to God we should follow this pattern. He pondered and studied the Word of

God. He allowed that teaching to grip him and then he sought to practise that Word by working it through every area of his life. But he didn't keep it all to himself. He passed it on to others. For Ezra it was not shallow teaching, it was substantiated by a credible lifestyle.

People will listen because they see the truth of the teaching demonstrated in someone's life. I fear that people don't listen to us because we say one thing with our lips but our lives say something else. But here is a man whose whole life was consistent. His mind was captivated by the truth of God. His practice was powered by that Word so that when he spoke to people it had an authentic note. Ezra is a model of how God wants us to live our lives. This verse is a pattern of what God requires of us all.

The last chapter of this book records a great revival under Ezra. He is usable because he is prepared. Are we usable (i.e. prepared)? Are we instruments that God could put his hand on and use right now? God sometimes uses the most unlikely people (Jonah, David, and Peter) in the Bible for the comfort of many like them. If we want our lives to count for something here is a man in the Old Testament who can teach us how to please God and live usable lives. Ezra found the secret of usefulness. He decided not to wander aimlessly but to live purposefully by setting his affection on the Scriptures, to know them and meditate on them. He was determined, by God's grace, to be what he should be by putting himself deliberately under the authority of the Word of God. This would be the rule of his life: that God would reign in his thinking and behaviour. We too need to respond to the challenge of God's Word if we are to be usable instruments in his hands for such a day as this.

Questions: for discussion

1. Why do you think that Ezra's preaching was persuasive?
2. How should we listen to preaching? Is it merely an aural experience or an activity that stimulates us to adopt certain attitudes and engage in appropriate action? Does 1 Tim 4:13 apply only to preachers or can it have an application to hearers of preaching? What lessons can we derive from James 1:22 about practical Christian living?
3. Ezra practised what he preached. Discuss the significance of this for every believer in the light of Ps. 51:10–13 and 2 Cor. 3:18.

4. What makes a Christian a credible witness of the gospel of grace?
5. How can we be usable instruments in God's hands?
6. What responsibilities do Christians (as custodians of the truth) have to the unconverted?

Trusting and testing the truth

Bible reading: Ezra 8

Focus on...

'I was ashamed to ask the king for soldiers and horsemen to protect us from enemies on the road, because we had told the king, "The gracious hand of our God is on everyone who looks to him, but his great anger is against all who forsake him.' (Ezra 8:22)

These are very honest words that reveal something of the character of Ezra. The people of God had been granted permission to return to Jerusalem. Ezra had made a very bold declaration concerning the providential care of God. He had told the king that God would protect them and punish anybody who incurred his wrath. He had proclaimed this great truth in faith and now he realised that he needed to possess it. There are times in the life of every preacher and every Christian when we are challenged to commit to the truth we are telling others. The thought of failure and humiliation may have crossed his mind but he was sure of his God. Surely the prayer of his heart would echo the psalmist, 'In you I trust, O my God. Do not let me be put to shame...' (Ps. 25:2).

There is an indication in our key verse that Ezra might have liked to ask the king for help. However, he was conscious that such a request would contradict the confident communication of the truth that the *'gracious hand of our God is on everyone who looks to him, but his great anger is against all who forsake him.'* In a sense he had trapped himself into a corner or perhaps we should say he had preached himself into a corner. Ezra was about to embark on a very important journey through dangerous terrain. He had responsibility for ensuring the safety of the people and their possessions and for the achievement of the objective to build the temple for the glory of God. He had gone out on a limb and had taken a risk but that act of faith was not a gamble. He realised that he had to trust the truth he had been teaching and the time had come to put it to the test. But in his heart he knew the truth that the psalmist declared, '*It is better to take refuge in the LORD than to trust in man. It is better to take refuge in the LORD than to trust in princes*' (Ps. 118:8–9).

'Let him who boasts boast in the Lord'

I believe this is where Ezra really took on the mantle of greatness. It was time to believe his beliefs. He had boasted about the might of his God to the king. The decision to not request the king to provide soldiers and horsemen for their protection, but to trust and test the truth of his teaching about God, shows us who Ezra really was. This is spiritual greatness! Some might see this decision as reckless in the face of such peril but he was primarily concerned with the glory of God. He had to be consistent in order not to compromise the honour of his great God. He was ashamed to ask the king for help because that would have been to publicly acknowledge that he really doubted the ability of God to safeguard the whole enterprise. He was not prepared to bring dishonour upon his God by taking out an insurance policy on his faith. The sentiment expressed by the psalmist was written on his heart, '*Some trust in chariots and some in horses, but we trust in the name of the LORD our God*' (Ps. 20:7).

We see that Ezra was prepared to depend on God, to go out on a limb and trust that God would take care of him. The Lord will bless those who trust in him: '*Blessed is the man who makes the LORD his trust…*' (Ps. 40:4). This truth is emphasised throughout Scripture and is encapsulated in Nahum 1:7, '*He cares for those who trust in him.*'

Our confidence in God must be real and evident to others both inside and outside the household of faith. It is particularly important that the leadership demonstrate such faith. Ezra was concerned for God's cause, God's reputation and God's glory. It is a disgrace for the people of God to live as if God is nothing more than a religious concept. God's people must demonstrate a living, dynamic dependence upon him. '*Woe to those who go down to Egypt for help, who rely on horses, who trust in the multitude of their chariots and in the great strength of their horsemen, but do not look to the Holy One of Israel, or seek help from the LORD*' (Is. 31:1). It is easy to say that we rely upon God and yet live a life of self-reliance. Learning to rely upon God and trusting and testing the truth in our experience is not merely something we are called on to do once in our lives. Neither is it something that we are called upon to do just once in a while. The real challenge in trusting God is to develop a lifestyle of regular and habitual dependence upon his providential care and to acknowledge that publicly.

Lessons in leadership from heroes of history

An active trust in the Lord will result in God's plans being prospered. Trust demands courage and courage, in turn, is a noble virtue. In the educational system of bygone days, people of history were held up as examples of noble character. The same is true of heroes in literature who were seen as role models for students who were being trained in character as well as intellect. Ezra is a man from whom we can learn a great deal. We can derive lessons in leadership from this great hero of history. One of the essential lessons we learn is that our trust in God will never be disappointed. It is most likely that Ezra *learned* to trust the Lord as he grew from spiritual infancy to maturity of faith. Our growth in the spiritual life is like that of the physical realm where children usually learn to crawl before taking baby steps. As they grow in confidence they learn to toddle and eventually to walk and run.

A good example of that courageous faith is given in the Old Testament account of David and Goliath. David, who was inexperienced in battle and relatively small in stature (compared with Goliath), stood before his gigantic opponent (a professional warrior) and said: *'You come against me with sword and spear and javelin, but I come against you in the name of the LORD Almighty, the God of the armies of Israel, whom you have defied'* (1 Sam. 17:45). Here is courage that has been strengthened in experience. The note of confidence comes from previous victories. It is not that David is self-confident, rather, it means that he has learned to trust his God. Thus we read that David persuaded Saul to allow him to face Goliath in battle with these words: *'The LORD who delivered me from the paw of the lion and the paw of the bear will deliver me from the hand of this Philistine'* (1 Sam. 17:37). Our trust in God will also grow stronger as it is strengthened in experience. As Christians we face an enemy who is far greater than us in strength but we do not face him with confidence in our own ability to overcome. Rather, we realise that the battle is not ours but the

Lord's and we trust the Word of the Lord spoken to Zerubbabel, 'Not by might nor by power, but by my Spirit,' says the LORD Almighty' (Zech. 4:6).

In the New Testament John reminds the believer of a great truth when he says, 'The one who is in you is greater than the one who is in the world' (1 John 4:4). Our trust, therefore, is in God alone and our experience tells us that he is dependable. In a world where people are becoming increasingly unreliable our confidence needs to be rooted in Christ. If we trust and test the truth we profess, as Ezra did, we will want to pause and erect a monument of praise to his power in preserving his people. Surely we too can say those great words spoken by Samuel when he took a stone and set it up and named it Ebenezer declaring, 'Thus far has the LORD helped us' (1 Sam. 7:12). He too was celebrating deliverance from the Philistine enemy. If we trust and test the truth of God's Word we will not only be preserved but we will prosper under the watchful care of our great God.

An outstanding example of that fearless trust in God is conveyed to us in the story of the three Hebrews, Shadrach, Meshach and Abednego who refused to obey King Nebuchadnezzar's decree to worship a golden image. They fearlessly proclaimed their trust in God and announced that he could deliver them. They also stated that the possibility that God might not intervene to redeem them from the fire would not deter them from their refusal to engage in idolatry. As we know, God intervened in a miraculous and very dramatic way. Their robes were not scorched, their hair was not singed, they were completely unharmed and there was not even the smell of smoke from their bodies!

God is able to protect and many believers will testify that the words of Isaiah have been true in their own experience: '...When you walk through the fire, you will not be burned; the flames will not set you ablaze' (Is. 43:2). There are times in the life of every child of God when we are called upon to trust and test the truth of these words. In difficult circumstances we may be fearful and we may feel the heat but he is faithful and he will be with us. He has never promised that we would not go through the fire, but he has promised to be with us.

However, history tells us that people have been burned for their faith. The flames that consumed the flesh of martyrs were neither quenched by prayer nor pitiful screaming. Many such martyrs had opportunity to recant their faith but preferred to die. They have left us an enduring example and a legacy of faith that is more precious than gold. If our generation is going to be one of purpose and destiny we need to trust and test the truth we profess irrespective of whatever that might cost.

Our trust in God needs to be established, unchanging and immovable. That solid faith is found in Job who had endured great affliction and yet could confidently proclaim, *'Though he slay me, yet will I hope in him...'* (Job 13:15).

Misplaced trust is a serious hindrance to faith. Goliath trusted in himself. Thus we read in 1 Samuel 17:42, *'He looked David over and saw that he was only a boy, ruddy and handsome, and he despised him.'* Our trust must be placed in our God, and confidence must come from who he is and not our own abilities and past achievements.

Every believer is faced with the issue of trusting God for safe-passage through territory that is potentially dangerous. The world in which we live has many distractions which would seek to lure us away from the route of our pilgrimage. Beelzebub has his bandits, and as a strategic tactician of spiritual warfare, he would seek to cut off the supply line and ambush us as we set our faces toward the territory that God is leading us into.

It is interesting to note that Nehemiah had a different attitude to Ezra insofar as he requested and accepted a military escort as part of God's benevolent care (see Neh. 2:7–9). We should bear in mind that Nehemiah was a political official as governor of Judah whereas Ezra was a priest on a spiritual mission. Their approach was, therefore, different. These are not contradictory positions as both men were acting with integrity by doing what they thought best in the circumstances and following the leading of the Lord. It was perfectly natural for the king to protect his official (Nehemiah) by providing a military escort, but Ezra felt he would have been inconsistent with his professed confidence in God (to protect his people and punish anybody who dared to attack them) to accept such assistance.

Faith is sometimes a matter of discretion when we are prompted by the Holy Spirit to adhere to a particular course (see Rom. 14:5–6). Ezra is being entirely consistent, therefore, when he says, *'I was ashamed to ask the king for soldiers and horsemen to protect us from enemies on the road, because we had told the king, "The gracious hand of our God is on everyone who looks to him, but his great anger is against all who forsake him"'* (8:22). He realised the seriousness of not accepting a military escort and that is shown in the subsequent verse, *'So we fasted and petitioned our God about this, and he answered our prayer'* (8:23). They were transporting a considerable amount of treasure that was assigned for use in the temple (see 8:24–30). Yet this cannot be construed as an ill-considered or flippant decision by a reckless leader. Ezra took the people to a place of complete dependence upon God. He dared to trust and test the truth and God honoured that decision. It gives us an insight into the character of the man and inspires us to rely more wholeheartedly on our God and the truth we profess.

The route of faith is presented as one that has dangers along the way but is safe if we trust God. The outcome was a safe journey to their destination and the outcome for those who trust themselves to his care today will be the same.

Questions: for discussion

1. Ezra trusted God. Was he reckless in not seeking safe passage from the king? Would it have been wiser to travel under military escort? How do you understand Ps. 20:7 and Is. 31:1?
2. See Ps. 25:2; Ps. 40:4; Ps. 118:8–9; Nahum 1:7. What do you think it means to rely upon God?
3. What does Ezra 8:22 tell us about the character of Ezra?
4. How can we exercise greater faith in what we profess to be true?
5. What impact does living and evident faith have on the message of the gospel in a godless society?
6. Is there any sense in which Is. 31:1 might apply to us in today's church?

Appalled by apostasy

Bible reading: Ezra 9

Focus on...

'I sat there appalled until the evening sacrifice.' (Ezra 9:4)

Imagine what life was like sixty years ago. Most of today's population was not even born then! Six decades is a span that separates one generation from another. So much can change in such a period of time. Sixty years had elapsed since the first group of people returned to Jerusalem under the leadership of Zerubbabel. When Ezra arrived in Jerusalem he learned of the sin of the people. They had failed to observe the clear command of God not to intermarry with the inhabitants of the region. They had not returned to idolatry but they had abandoned the rule of God's Word in certain areas of their lives. He did not learn of this issue immediately. The drastic measures dealing with the issue of intermarriage were announced four and a half months after his arrival.

The main offenders were the leaders of the people. How sad this is, and it is a reminder to us all that those who have responsibility for leading the people of God must do so by example. In a sense they were still leading the people, but they were leading them astray instead of leading them in the ways of the Lord. Ezra was appalled by the apostasy of the people. He literally tore his hair out with grief and sat in silent mourning and astonishment. The people had continued to observe the external rituals of worship and it seems they did so with a certain degree of sincerity. However, they were in breach of the explicitly stated decree of the Lord to not intermarry with the heathen peoples. This clear command is recorded in Deuteronomy 7:1–3: *'When the LORD your God brings you into the land you are entering to possess and drives out before you many nations— the Hittites, Girgashites, Amorites, Canaanites, Perizzites, Hivites and Jebusites, seven nations larger and stronger than you—and when the*

LORD *your God has delivered them over to you and you have defeated*
them, then you must destroy them totally. Make no treaty with them, and
show them no mercy. Do not intermarry with them. Do not give your
daughters to their sons or take their daughters for your sons...'

Is sin still shocking?

Now these were the very peoples that God's people had intermarried with
(9:1–2). Ezra was appalled and shocked by their disobedience. How we
need men like Ezra today who will see the true standards of righteousness
required of God's people and not be content to settle for less. He was
offended and grieved in his heart to learn that the *'holy race'* had
compromised. Their action is rightly described as *'unfaithfulness'* (9:2). I
wonder how the leaders and the people who had intermarried justified their
behaviour? There may have been a disparity between the numbers of men
and available Jewish women who returned from exile. In any case they had
not only accommodated such practices but they had indulged in them
themselves: *'The leaders and officials have led the way in this*
unfaithfulness' (9:2). This behaviour was an expression of unfaithfulness
to their covenant with God.

Ezra went before God in prayer and he unburdened his soul to the Lord.
It is an amazing prayer that begins with personal confession and develops
into intercessory prayer on behalf of the people. He identifies himself with
the people as he prays *'our guilt...our sins'* (9:7). He recalls the history of
Israel, their failure and sinfulness and the catastrophic consequences. Then
he recounts the grace of God in allowing a remnant to return from Babylon.
He is overwhelmed with sorrow and casts himself and the people on the
mercy of God. He does not, in fact, petition God for deliverance! It is true
confession marked with *'godly sorrow [that] brings repentance...'* (2 Cor.
7:10). There was no plea bargaining, no attempt to explain any mitigating
circumstances because he was keenly aware that there are no circumstances
on which to appeal for greater leniency. Without this true sense of
sinfulness we can never fully appreciate grace! He identifies himself with
sinners because he knew his God to be a righteous God. In the light of such
knowledge he was all too aware that he too was a miserable sinner who
needed the grace of God.

Carnality begins with carelessness

Although the people had not engaged in idolatry they were moving in that direction. That is why God prohibited intermarriage. He commanded, *'Do not intermarry with them. Do not give your daughters to their sons or take their daughters for your sons, for they will turn your sons away from following me to serve other gods'* (Deut. 7:3–4). God clearly stated that the outcome of such unholy unions would be apostasy. There are so many people today who think they know better than God does! God's people today need to recapture the sense that they are a 'holy race'. As a minister I have heard people tell me that they wish to marry their non-Christian girlfriend or boyfriend. In spite of the counsel of God's Word they are determined to pursue such a course of action. God is sovereign and I believe he can overrule in all situations, but generally, it has to be said that such marriages are inappropriate and destined to be unhelpful in the spiritual life of the believer. Somehow the optimism of love and youth blinds them to the truth of God's Word. They believe they can influence the unsaved partner and 'lead her or him to the Lord'. In my experience that is a very unlikely outcome. What happens, almost invariably, is that the non-Christian partner has a detrimental influence on the believer!

An important principle to learn in the spiritual life is that corruption and carnality begin with carelessness. I have very rarely seen a Christian suddenly and dramatically abandon faith, although it does happen. What is all too common, however, is the process of backsliding. Where does it begin? Apathy leads to apostasy and the ultimate outcome of indifference may very well be idolatry! God's people at the time of Ezra were well on the road to idolatry even though they may not have realised it or perhaps they would have strenuously denied any such inference. But we are called to believe God, and he said that idolatry would be the inevitable outcome of intermarriage.

Their decline began with laxity and compromise. Sacrifices were intended to make provision for lapses into disobedience, but had they become a substitute for disobedience itself? It seems that they were engaged in ritual techniques for keeping God happy rather than true, obedient religion. Is there a parallel with the people of God today? Is it possible that we go through the motions of church attendance and even our quiet times in this manner while disobeying the truth revealed to us in his Word? I am afraid that it is all too easy to engage in self-deceiving rituals. Sadly, today we see the abuse of God's grace and the attitude seems to be that it is better to sin and seek forgiveness than to submit to the authority of Scripture. What an abuse of grace!

Dead religion

Genuine worship can deteriorate into mechanical observance of religious practices. This is not merely something that happened in the history of Israel. These events in Ezra are not recorded simply as an interesting historical cameo about God's people in the past. That is why Paul told Timothy, 'All scripture is God-breathed and is useful for teaching, rebuking, correcting and training in righteousness' (2 Tim. 3:16). There are present day parallels and we must seek to apply the message of Ezra as we explore its content.

With God's people returning to Jerusalem and re-establishing temple worship, one might well think that they were vulnerable to attack in the midst of surrounding heathen nations. However, it was not attack but decline through intermarriage, which posed the greatest threat. It seems to me that the situation is the same in every generation. We must, therefore, be careful to deploy our defence resources where they are most needed. Although many people are attracted to false religions and cults, it has to be said that very few Christians ever join their ranks. What is far more likely to happen, and is in fact already happening, is that believers are flirting with prevailing worldviews and many are married to materialism. We may fear external enemies but the enemy is within our own hearts. We are far more susceptible to decline from within than succumbing to attack from without.

Consider spiritual health in terms of a continuum (a straight line) and put good spiritual health at the left end and poor spiritual health at the right end of that line. Where, along that line, would you position the church today? What becomes clear when we look at things in those graphic terms is that moving from a position of positive strength to a position of weakness is a gradual process. That journey is taken in small steps. Therefore we need to be alert to the subtle shifts. When we do this, of course we will be accused of being paranoid and people will say that we are preoccupied with heresy hunting. But there are early warning signs of decline in the lives of individuals and the life of the church. It often begins with a lowering of standards. How do Christians come to hate other Christians? It begins with something that is less than the love to which we are called to give expression and ultimately leads to bitterness. The Word of God is not only like a thermometer for taking the temperature of the church but more than that it is like a thermostat for regulating the temperature of the church.

Inconsistency

Chapter nine of Ezra draws attention to the contrast between the holy vocation of Israel and its unholy conduct. These marriages were irreconcilable with the calling of Israel. As we seek to apply the message of Ezra to our contemporary situation we must ask: are our lifestyles at variance with our calling and holy vocation in Christ? They had displeased God by disobeying his Word. They were chosen for a purpose and intermarriage ran counter to that purpose. A wife or husband is a soul mate and marriage has a solemn religious dimension. It cannot, therefore, be seen as just a convenient or expedient social arrangement.

Believers are strenuously warned against forming unholy alliances. Paul wrote, 'Do not be unequally yoked together with unbelievers. For what fellowship has righteousness with lawlessness? And what communion has light with darkness? And what accord has Christ with Belial? Or what part has a believer with an unbeliever? And what agreement has the temple of God with idols? For you are the temple of the living God. As God has said: "I will dwell in them and walk among them. I will be their God, and they shall be my people"' (2 Cor. 6:14–16 NKJV). This is not an injunction against any and all associations with unbelievers, but any relationship with unbelievers which could compromise godly standards or jeopardise consistency of Christian witness, especially, though not exclusively, marriage. It is an injunction that would apply equally to dubious business partnerships. It is a clear prohibition against forming close attachments with non-Christians or anything that involves compromise with godlessness.

The five rhetorical questions in this passage all presuppose a negative answer. They stress the incompatibility of Christianity with alternative worldviews or religions. Thus the case is made and the incongruity of intimate relationships with unbelievers is identified for what it is, absurd and abominable.

The chief reason why believers must not enter any compromising relationship with unbelievers is that they belong exclusively to God. We are the temple or sanctuary of the living God. In marriage, God's people must not be unequally yoked. They must respect their Christian obligations and privileges to marry in the Lord. The neglect of this principle has caused misery and apostasy and many have condemned themselves to lives of life-long sorrow.

One of the great privileges of marriage where that marriage is blessed with children is to lead children to faith, wholeness and maturity in Christ. As the psalmist says, *'Behold, children are a heritage from the Lord, The fruit of the womb is a reward'* (Ps. 127:3 NKJV). The people of God are to raise their children in the knowledge of the things of God and do all they can to nurture their children in the ways of the Lord. How can a believer ever expect the non-believer to share that perspective on the diverse range of issues that they will face? It is impossible! The question asked in Amos 3:3 seems particularly appropriate, *'Do two walk together unless they have agreed to do so?'* The obvious answer is no, they cannot because there needs to be agreement about the direction, the pace, the destination, etc. It seems that many of God's people today see marriage to non-believers as something akin to a cross-cultural marriage. No doubt cross-cultural marriages between two believers may present additional challenges, but there is no comparison simply because the marriage of a believer to a non-believer is forbidden.

Accommodating apostasy

It is difficult to understand how some evangelical ministers are prepared to officiate at such marriage ceremonies. The argument often used is that 'the couple was going to get married anyway, and I used whatever influence I had to deter them. Failing that I took the opportunity to present marriage in a Christian context.' One might have heard pastors say they had wonderful opportunity to explain the gospel and discuss pertinent issues such as communication, finance, sex, parenting and so on. It seems to me that pragmatism sometimes pushes our principles aside. I'm not questioning their integrity but our judgement must be based on scriptural principles. Ministers need the grace and wisdom of God in such situations. I love my fellow ministers in Christ and I do not condemn them if they have acted as I describe above, but I would ask them to consider this perspective which I commend to them in love. I believe that to seek to solemnise a marriage between a Christian and a non-Christian in the eyes of society is inappropriate. Is it right before heaven? It is not sectarianism to preach against modern day intermarriage; rather, it is a much-needed fidelity to Scripture.

Paul actually encouraged the Christian partner in a mixed marriage to maintain the relationship as long as possible (1 Cor. 7:12–16). He was speaking to people who were married before they were converted to Christianity. This passage applies to a situation, therefore, where one partner may be converted after marriage. The clear implication for today is that in such circumstances there cannot be any legitimate basis for an appeal for divorce on such grounds. Marriage is not to be treated lightly.

The heathen women of the surrounding nations may well have retained a natural longing for the indulgences of their own religion and they could lead their husbands into compliance with their desires. Ultimately they could lead their husbands into idolatry. Their covenant relationship to God had both vertical and lateral dimensions. Their relationship to God is the obvious vertical dimension but their horizontal relationships to each other also constituted an important part of the covenant triangle. To violate their relationship to one another was to violate their relationship to him. Psalm 106 catalogues the evil practices of God's people throughout their turbulent history and includes, '...*they mingled with the nations and adopted their customs*' (Ps. 106:35).

The church needs men who are appalled by apostasy, men who are prepared to confess their sinfulness before God and to intercede in prayer for the mercy of the Almighty in our generation. We have become too accustomed to low standards of morality, de-sensitised by the media and influenced by the prevailing moral climate of today. Even people within the church think that it is only cranks and crackpots that expect such exacting standards. Ezra was God's man for that generation. His response to the sinfulness of God's people reflected the true awfulness of sin and surely that is how the Lord saw it. Isn't that how God still sees sin today?

Ezra's reaction was not extreme; it was entirely appropriate. In fact Nehemiah when he encountered the same problem did not tear his own hair out (as Ezra did). On the contrary he rebuked them, beat them, tore out their hair and made them take an oath that they would never again intermarry (Neh. 13:25). Nehemiah saw that the men of Judah had married heathen women and he records that *'half of their children spoke the language of Ashdod or the language of one of the other peoples, and did not know how to speak the language of Judah'* (13:24). Therein lies the tragedy, whatever their intentions may have been the reality speaks for itself. They had been assimilated into godless culture and the sins of the fathers were surely visited upon the children. The issue of intermarriage is recorded always as an issue where serious spiritual decline begins. The eternal lesson for God's people is that there cannot be areas of our lives which we deem to be outside the spiritual influence of God's Word. Ezra recognised apostasy when he saw it and he was so in tune with the heart of the Almighty that he was appalled and moved to intercession. I trust that will be our attitude inspiring us to intercessory action.

Questions: for discussion

1. Why was Ezra appalled? See Deut. 7:1–4.
2. Where does backsliding begin? Where does it end?
3. Why should Christians marry Christians? Why should a Christian not marry an unbeliever? See 2 Cor. 6:14–16.
4. What is the appropriate attitude for a Christian partner in a mixed marriage? See 1Cor. 7:12–16.
5. Does the sin that surrounds us not grieve us? See Acts 17:16–34.
6. Was Ezra too severe in his handling of this situation of intermarriage?

Contrition, confession and the cost of compromise

Bible reading: Ezra 10

Focus on...

'Then Ezra the priest stood up and said to them, "You have been unfaithful; you have married foreign women, adding to Israel's guilt. Now make confession to the LORD, the God of your fathers, and do his will. Separate yourselves from the peoples around you and from your foreign wives." The whole assembly responded with a loud voice: "You are right! We must do as you say."' (Ezra 10:10–12)

This was a courageous act on the part of Ezra. To delve into family matters is always dangerous and to seek to disentangle the familial ties of these people required great fortitude. However, he had the support of the people (10:4) and so 'he put the leading priests and Levites and all Israel under oath to do what had been suggested' (10:5). Ezra led a great revival. Where does revival begin? Not in the hearts of people as some suppose but in heaven. It begins when the Holy Spirit quickens the hearts of his people by bringing about that sorrow which draws us to repentance. The people were truly contrite. They admitted their guilt and confessed their sin. It is only in this condition of repentance that God restores and rewards. Revival is a sovereign activity, we cannot invoke it either by prayer or piety or any other means. But if we want God to be active in our midst we must at least fulfil the conditions he desires which create a climate for it. The light of his awesome glory should reveal the terrible depravity of sin and bring a conviction of the need for total cleansing.

Attitude and authority

Ezra influenced the people by his attitude rather than his authority. His example was a compelling testimony to the truth that they had ignored and they were convicted and contrite. But there is a cost contingent upon that contrition. They must put matters right. They could not merely feel sorry and continue as before after a period of mourning. Action had to be taken to address the matter. Although Ezra had support it was not unanimous. There were those who disagreed with the proposed course of action to separate from the women and children of these intermarriages. Four people (one of them a Levite!) opposed the proposed remedy (10:15). In fact, it was Ezra who supported the suggestion of the people. But he did have the responsibility for seeing that their undertaking to correct the situation was fulfilled and it was he who inspired them to think of their behaviour in the light of God's Word.

This is not an act of vicarious repentance (there is no such thing). Each person must repent individually as verse one shows: 'While Ezra was praying and confessing, weeping and throwing himself down before the house of God, a large crowd of Israelites—men, women and children— gathered around him. They too wept bitterly.' Ezra's mourning and prayer enabled the people to become aware of the seriousness of their sin. Shecaniah then acknowledged their wrongdoing and proposed a solution. He exhorted Ezra to take courageous action, and on behalf of the people he pledged support. It is at this point that Ezra called on the people to put things right with God. Drastic action was needed to make a clean breast of things and so the inappropriate marriages were annulled. Thus the people were restored to their separateness. The result of repentance is restoration.

Adhering to the word in adversity

Can you imagine the day of separation when it came? Chapter ten does not record the details besides listing the names of those who were guilty of intermarriage. As such it is a very effective understatement. It must have been a harrowing experience. It may be seen as a passage where the exacting standards of a righteous God have to be met. However, it should be remembered that it was the sinfulness of these people that led to such a terrible situation. I have no doubt that it was a traumatic experience for everybody and not just those who had intermarried. Friendships must have developed between people and families and now those relationships too had to be severed. It is impossible to read this chapter of *Ezra* without feeling moved. Did Ezra lack compassion? Considering the fact that these marriages were well established, and taking into account that there were children involved, could he not have been more inventive in framing a solution? Could he not have said 'all that is in the past' and been content that they confessed their sins? Could he not have suggested that in future no such action would be permitted and resolve to impose severe sanctions on any who behaved in this manner henceforth? Does the action seem draconian? Where is the mercy? Where is the forgiveness? What kind of heart could not be moved to clemency in such circumstances? I wonder if those who opposed the measures suggested that he was callous. I wonder if his critics said that he was putting grand principles before the problems of real people.

If we say it about Ezra then we must be consistent and say the same about God! Will we question his judgement in putting Adam and Eve out of the Garden of Eden? Will we accuse him of lacking compassion? Will we say he is altogether too severe? Will we argue that clemency would have been more appropriate? Will we plead that there should have been a second chance? Will we ask where is the forgiveness? Will we dare to say that God's action was calloused? Will we ask if he could not have been more creative in finding a less drastic solution? Will we ask if he could not have set aside his noble principles for a moment and handled the problem in a manner more conducive to the needs of the people concerned?

Ezra was acting in accordance with God's Word, which he knew so very well. It was action that averted the wrath of God by availing of his mercy. In fact when we examine the facts we see that those who had intermarried represented a very small minority. We are given the details and if we care to work them out we find that in percentage terms those who intermarried represented 0.22%. Chapter two informs us: *'The whole company numbered 42,360, besides their 7,337 menservants and maidservants; and they also had 200 men and women singers'* (vv. 64–65). When we add those numbers together we get a total of 50,797. Chapter ten closes with the list of the one hundred and twelve names of those who had intermarried and this represents 0.22%. Yet it must be said that the problem was widespread insofar as it involved a wide range of groups (10:18–44). It was yeast that would contaminate the whole loaf. The greater good of the nation had to be considered, and above all else, obedience to the commands of God had to be foremost.

The last verse of *Ezra* tells us, *'All these had married foreign women, and some of them had children by these wives'* (10:44). So there could not have been a huge number of children involved. However, one feels that even one child was one too many. This is the cost of contrition. God had spoken and no human act could legitimise the situation. To seek to do so would have been entirely wrong. Thus Ezra is to be commended not criticised.

The banished and the blessed

In chapter three of this book, 'The Lord's List', we noted that the Holy Spirit chose to put on record the names of the tribes, clans and families of all those who took the opportunity to return from Babylon to Jerusalem. Now in the closing chapter of Ezra there is another list. If the former list is to be seen as a scroll of honour then the latter list must be seen as a scroll of dishonour. Man tends to record his achievements and forget his failures, as evidenced in the fact that we have scrolls of honour in our communities, but when did you last see a scroll of dishonour? Again the point is reinforced that God is a God of detail and he keeps records. The books will be balanced one day and those whose names are written in the Lamb's Book of Life will live for eternity in his glorious presence. Those names which are not found in that book will suffer eternal separation and conscious punishment. The record is written in the indelible blood of Christ and cannot be fraudulently adjusted. He is the eternal auditor!

Surely our hearts ache as we read this passage to see God's people once again putting themselves into a situation that had very painful consequences. We can only imagine the unbearable grief that they experienced in parting with their families forever. Their consciousness of the sinfulness of these intermarriage relationships outweighed the affection of their hearts. Surely that tells us a great deal about the depth of sorrow that led to their repentance. Not only did their sin have profound personal implications, but it also had serious social consequences. They ruined the lives of many women and children. The resentment stirred up in the hearts of the extended families to which they belonged must have been very great indeed. The consequence of sin is always awful for all those affected by it.

Christ was cursed so that we might be commended to God

It is difficult to part with loved ones. Yet God sent his only begotten Son into the world to take away the sin of the world. He had committed no sin and there was no sinfulness in his nature. Yet in the triune counsel of the Godhead it was agreed that Christ would leave the realms of glory, take on human flesh, suffer and die, despised and rejected by men and even forsaken by God the Father. In this sad scene in Ezra when it was time to part there must have been tears and heartbreaking cries. But was there ever a cry more heartbreaking than that from the cross when Christ called out, 'Eloi, Eloi, lama sabachthani?'—which means, 'My God, my God, why have you forsaken me?' (Matt. 27:46).

All those who trust in Christ alone, by faith alone will enter the vicarious victory wrought for them at Calvary. May the Holy Spirit bring about a conviction of sin that leads to contrition and confession! Because it is only out of such repentance that restoration of right relationship with God may take place.

Questions: for discussion

1. What do we learn about Ezra and his style of leadership from Ezra 10:1?
2. Why should we see Ezra as courageous in the way he dealt with the issue of intermarriage?
3. Sin may have serious social consequences. Discuss in the light of Ezra 10:44.
4. The awesome glory of God reveals the terrible depravity of sin and brings a conviction of the need for total cleansing. See Is. 6:1–6. What can these verses teach us about self-awareness and 'self-esteem' in relation to the perfect holiness of God?
5. Read Matt. 27:27–50 and consider the crucifixion of Christ. What does it tell us about the seriousness of sin?
6. What does it mean to trust in the completed work of Christ alone for your salvation? See Eph. 2:8–10.

Select bibliography

Commentaries on Ezra

Breneman, Mervin, *The New American Commentary: Ezra Nehemiah and Esther* (Broadman and Holman, 1993).

Fensham, Charles, F., *New International Commentary on the Old Testament: The Books of Ezra and Nehemiah* (Eerdmans, 1982).

Keil, C.F., *The Books of Ezra, Nehemiah and Esther* (Eerdmans, 1970).

Kidner, Derek, *Tyndale Old Testament Commentaries: Ezra and Nehemiah* (IVP, 1979).

Williamson, H.G.M., *Word Biblical Commentary: Ezra, Nehemiah* (Word Inc., 1985).

Bibliographic Surveys

Carson, D.A., *New Testament Commentary Survey* (Baker, 1986).

Spurgeon, Charles H., *Commenting and Commentaries* (Banner of Truth 1969).

Wiersbe, Warren W., *A Basic Library for Bible Students* (Baker, 1981).

One-Volume Commentaries on the Whole Bible

Guthrie, Donald, J. A. Motyer, A.M. Stibbs and D. J. Wiseman, eds., *The New Bible Commentary: Revised*. 3rd edition (Eerdmans, 1970).

Harrison, E.F., and Charles F. Pfeiffer, *The Wycliffe Bible Commentary* (Moody, 1962).

Henry, Matthew, *Matthew Henry's Commentary on the Whole Bible* (Hendrickson, 1991).

Commentary Sets

Calvin, John, *Calvin's Commentaries*. 22 vols (Baker, 1981).

Gaebelein, Frank E., general ed., *The Expositor's Bible Commentary*. 12 vols. (1978).

Harrison, R.K. (1968–1993) and Robert L. Hubbard, Jr. (1994–), *The New International Commentary on the Old Testament*.

Hubbard David A. and Glenn W. Barker (Old Testament Editor John D. W. Watts), *Word Biblical Commentary* (1985).

Keil, C. F. and F. Delitzsch, *Biblical Commentary on the Old Testament.* 11 vols (Eerdmans, 1968).
Wiseman, D.J., ed., *The Tyndale Old Testament Commentaries* (IVP).

General Reference
Bromiley, Geoffrey W., ed., *The International Standard Bible Encyclopaedia.* 4 vols. (Eerdmans, 1979–1988).
Douglas, J. D., ed., *The New Bible Dictionary,* 2nd. ed. (Tyndale, 1982).
Ferguson, Sinclair B., David F. Wright and J. I. Packer, *New Dictionary of Theology* (IVP, 1988).

Concordances Expository Dictionaries and Interlinears
Kohlenberger III, John R., *The Interlinear NIV Hebrew-English Old Testament* (Zondervan, 1979).
Strong, James. *Exhaustive Concordance of the Bible* (Abingdon, 1980).
Vine, W.E. Merrill F. Unger and William White Jr., *Vines Complete Expository Dictionary of Old and New Testament Words* (Thomas Nelson, 1984).
Young, Robert, ed., *Analytical Concordance to the Bible* (Revised edition, 1980).

Hermeneutics
Fee, G.D. and Stuart, D., *How to Study the Bible for all its Worth* (SU, 1984).
Berkof L., *Principles of Biblical Intepretation* (Baker Book House, 1977).
Bray, Gerald, *Biblical Interpretation Past & Present* (IVP Apollos, 1996).
Carson, D. A. & Woodbridge, John D. (eds.), *Scripture & Truth* (IVP, 1983).
Fee, G. D., *Listening to the Spirit in the Text* (Eerdmans, 2000).
Goldsworthy, Graeme, *According to Plan* (IVP, 1991).
Marshall, I.H. (ed.), *New Testament Interpretation* (Paternoster, 1977. Reprinted in the Biblical and Theological Classics series 1997).
Mickelson, A.B., *Interpreting the Bible* (Eerdmans, 1970).
Motyer, Steve, *The Bible with Pleasure,* (Crossway, S.U. 1990. Reprinted 2000).

Select bibliography

Osborne, Grant R., *The Hermeneutical Spiral* (IVP USA, 1991).
Reid, A., *Postcard from Palestine* (St Matthias Media, 2nd edition, 1997).
Sproul, R.C., *Knowing God's Word* (Ark Publishing, 1977).
Stibbs, A., *Understanding God's Word* (IVP, 1976).
Stott, John, *Understanding the Bible* (IVP, 1972).
Tan, Paul Lee, *The Interpretation of Prophecy* (BMH, 1974).
Terry, Milton S., *Biblical Hermeneutics* (Zondervan, 1974).

Theological Works

Berkhof, L., *Systematic Theology* (Eerdmans, 1984).
Erickson, Millard J., *Christian Theology*, 3 vols. (Baker 1983–85).
Kaiser, Walter C., *Toward an Exigetical Theology: Biblical Exegesis for Preaching and Teaching* (Baker, 1981).
Murray, John, *Collected Writings of John Murray*, 4 vols. (Banner of Truth, 1976–1982).
Warfield, Benjamin B., *Biblical and Theological Studies* (Presbyterian and Reformed, 1968).